Praise for *Ciao, America!*

"Witty . . . Whatever you have taken for granted in America is what Severgnini observes with the freshness and charm of the outsider, here for an extended visit. He gives us back ourselves—with our manners and mores and even the fine print on our No Parking signs—in a shining mirror." —*Philadelphia Weekly Press*

"*Ciao, America!* reads like Alexis de Tocqueville reincarnated with a sense of humor. Beppe Severgnini is not only wickedly witty, he is an astute and intelligent observer of the American way of life. A wonderful and uplifting book." —Nelson DeMille

"It would be difficult not to like this delightful book." —*Library Journal*

"A delight . . . a laugh-a-minute chain of funny anecdotes." —*Boston Herald*

"It's not easy to walk the thin line between Tocqueville's *Democracy in America* and *Dave Barry's Only Travel Guide You'll Ever Need*, but this memoir manages to do so admirably." —*Booklist*

"I'm afraid that we Americans may not *deserve* a commentator as witty, generous, and perceptive as Mr. Severgnini; his attention, his sympathy, and his prose are a kind of grace, abounding." —Michael Chabon

"*Ciao, America!* is fun from first page to last." —*Chicago Sun-Times*

Ciao, America!

An Italian Discovers the U.S.

BEPPE SEVERGNINI

Translated by Giles Watson

BROADWAY BOOKS

New York

BROADWAY

A hardcover edition of this book was originally published in 2002 by
Broadway Books.

An English-language edition of this book was published under the title *An Italian in America* in 2001 by R.C.S. Libri & Grandi Opere
S.p.A., Via Mecenate, 91 20138 Milano, ITALY.

PRINTED IN THE UNITED STATES OF AMERICA

Visit our website at www.broadwaybooks.com

First Broadway Books trade paperback edition published 2003

Book design by Julie Duquet

The Library of Congress has cataloged the hardcover edition as follows:
Severgnini, Beppe.
  [Italiano in America, English]
  Ciao, America! : an Italian discovers the U.S. / Beppe
Severgnini ; translated by Giles Watson.— 1st Broadway Books ed.
  p. cm.
  1. United States—Social life and customs—1971– 2. United
States—Description and travel. 3. Severgnini, Beppe—Journeys—
United States. 4. Italians—Travel—United States. I. Title.
E169.04 .S48 2002
917.304'931—dc21   2001052649

ISBN 0-7679-1236-5

10   9   8   7   6   5

To Antonio

Contents

Ciao, America!

Introduction

It seemed to me that only in such a peaceful, slightly old-fashioned place could one catch America unawares and find out what Americans were really like.

LUIGI BARZINI, *O America!*

Italians who come to America arrive with an Italian head.

GIUSEPPE PREZZOLINI,
America in pantofole

THIS BOOK IS the product of prolonged inexperience. It's the story of a year spent in the United States, a country, as I came to realize, that you are completely unprepared for when you arrive. Everything I had learned in the course of many previous visits was no help at all. The American news we are bombarded with in Europe is like having a searchlight shine directly into your eyes: there's plenty of light but you can't see anything. Ordinary America—the country you enter as you come out of the airport, unless you're particularly unfortunate—is one of the world's best-kept secrets.

I have understood the most important things about this country—that is if I've understood anything at all—just by sitting tight and watching. There is, I was fascinated to find out, an America that goes wild about ice, that thinks discretionary tips are mandatory, that worships at the shrine of air-conditioning, and performs arcane rituals in honor of the fiendish god of the easy chair. It's an America of strange noises, strong flavors, and faint smells. That everyday America, in my view, is crucial. But few have attempted to explain how it works.

I am offering the reader a chance to explore it with me. I spent twelve months, from one spring to the next, in a small house in Georgetown, an old neighborhood where Washington turns into a normal city. It's the right place to ask your first questions (why don't they turn the air-conditioning down?) and get those first all-important answers (because that's the way they like it). Georgetown is the ideal setting in which to join battle with a plumber called Marx, to be ambushed by a seriously laconic mailperson and to be besieged by thoughtful neighbors.

Some readers may remember that in previous books I have stalked Italians abroad, spied on Eastern Europeans, and subjected the British to scrutiny. Well, it wasn't easy going from Britain, where hot means lukewarm, to America, where the same word means incandescent. And experiencing at firsthand the local sense of humor was equally traumatic. In the USA there is no such thing as understatement. If you say "I'm not very good" in Great Britain, it really means "I'm fantastic." If Americans are good at something (work, sport, sex), they come right out and tell you.

Most of the surprises were pleasant ones, though. I found out that children run things around here and that death is considered optional. I tried my hand at computer shopping, I got lost in car parks, I fought tooth and nail (failing) to acquire a credit card. I celebrated the Fourth of July. I chased a possum through my shrubbery. And I discussed politics with a neighbor called Greg. I realized why people care about neon, that soother of American angst, and I investigated the local passion for gadgets, which should not be underestimated. In its search to perfect the pocket-sized and portable, this country has covered a lot of ground.

As I was rereading this book, I became aware that my vision of America had come gradually into focus. The stupor of the early months gave way to a certain number of conclusions (right or wrong—I'll let you be the judge of that). I decided to keep that sense of progressive discovery because I think it is the attitude many Italians—indeed, many Europeans—have toward the United States. Naturally, some of my compatriots get off the plane convinced that they know everything, but they're a minority (the same minority that knows all there is to know about politics, football, and wine). But most are happy to watch, learn, and comment (as soon as they find anyone willing to listen).

There is one thing I'd like to say to them: the discovery of America—which is as complicated today as it was in 1492—doesn't depend on how many miles you drive, or the number of states you've been to. America reveals itself in the little things. And to discover them, you need the inquisitiveness of a new arrival and the patience of a beachcomber, one of those mildly inappropriate individuals who roam the shores in search of small treasures. The seashore is America. The mildly inappropriate individual is me. Wish me luck, and let's get combing.

Washington, April 1995

April

*O*ur house is made of white wood and faces west. The black-painted door has a fan carved above it and the shutters of the three windows are nailed back in case some prudish European should think of closing them at night.

At the back, hidden from the street, is a garden with an ivy-covered lawn. In the midst of the ivy, like a mermaid rising from the waves, is a concrete cupid. The owners may have hoped that Washington winters would make it look antique, but if that was the case, they are going to have to wait a little longer. For the time being, the concrete cupid still looks like a cupid made of concrete and continues to pour imaginary water from a concrete jug while staring in open hostility at the world round about—squirrels, blackbirds, and the occasional Italian tenant.

The house is on Thirty-fourth Street, which runs one way downhill through Georgetown. Actually, Thirty-fourth Street itself is a curious thoroughfare. It's only busy from four to six in the afternoon, when the massed office staffs of Washington descend toward M Street and cross the Potomac over Key Bridge on their way home to the immaculate suburbs of North Virginia. For the remaining twenty-two hours of the day, Thirty-fourth Street is a quiet road of brightly painted houses where people call each other by their first names and pretend that Georgetown is still the sleepy village that used to make a living from the tobacco trade at the time of the Revolution.

Apart from a certain number of lawyers, who in America are practically ubiquitous, our stretch of Thirty-fourth Street, from Volta Place to P Street, boasts an allergy specialist, a clerk at the World Bank, the daughter of a former CIA agent, a senator from Montana, and five exquisitely polite students from New England, whom I have unsuccessfully encouraged to behave like John Belushi in the film *Animal House*. Dave, their spokesperson, gently hinted that it would be undignified for a young American to humor a foreigner's fantasies.

Georgetown is known officially as West Washington, a name that is used by no one. It extends over one square mile and has had a checkered history. When there is a Democrat in the White House (Kennedy, Carter, Clinton), its stock rises, only to fall when the Republicans move in (Nixon, Reagan, Bush). Conservatives prefer the quiet of the suburbs to the Bohemian lifestyle of the center. In the western part of Georgetown, near the river Potomac, lies the university, founded by Jesuits in the eighteenth century. To the east, beyond the lights of Wisconsin Avenue, the houses are larger and older. In the center are the dwellings that once belonged to artisans or traders. We live in the center.

These cramped, dark houses with their steep staircases are about as un-American as you could possibly imagine. A farmer from Oklahoma might use one for keeping poultry. In fact, Washington's propertied classes do exactly the same thing, only their chickens come from the far side of the Atlantic. Yes, we Europeans love houses like these to distraction. In a detached suburban house, we might risk feeling we were actually living in America but the tiny rooms and woodworm-riddled floors of Georgetown serve to cushion the blow of moving from the Old World. We are prepared to pay a premium for inconvenience of this caliber. The agencies know it and take full advantage.

• • •

FINDING A HOUSE with just the right degree of discomfort among so many inconvenient homes was not easy. Knowing that we would only be staying in the United States for a year, our first thoughts were to go for a furnished residence. These do exist in Washington but the problem is the furniture. In the course of a week-long search—in the company of a certain Ellen, who kept telling us not to worry, thus increasing our anxiety—we inspected a number of bizarre places. Selected highlights include: a basement flat decked out like a Bavarian castle, complete with hunting trophies; a six-floor house on P Street with one room per floor; a house decorated in purple throughout, including the bathroom and kitchen; and a house in Glover Park where the only thing missing to shoot a horror film was a suitable victim. Us, presumably.

Naturally, we changed tack and looked at unfurnished accommodation, which in America is the norm. Americans take everything with them when they move, like tortoises. Anything they can't carry is sold, thrown away or put into storage. Our search was carried out in the small ads of the *Washington Post* and operational headquarters were set up in the kitchen of some British friends, who helped us to decipher the more intriguing prospects. For example, what does this mean?

NE—3br, 1½ ba semi-det, w/w cpt, eat-in kit, Sect 8 welcome

Who are the initiates of "Sect 8"? And why didn't the owner of

GEO'TN 3br, 2½ ba, spac, renv TH, Pkg, WD, Lg-trm lse

spend a couple of dollars more and buy a few vowels? Or what on earth can you say about

GEO'TWN Classic 3br TH, fpl, gdn, plus guest or au-pair?

Did the owner want to rent us a guest or an au-pair? And what about that "classic"? This is the country where classic is a kind of Coca-Cola. So, thanks anyway, but no.

In the end, just as our British friends were becoming discreetly desperate, we found

GEO'TWN Grace and charm. 3br, 3½ ba, immac, lib, cac, lg gdn. Ph Ms Webb.

The crucial information here is not *3br* (three monastery cell–sized bedrooms), nor is it *3½ ba* (three and a half bathrooms that, added together, are smaller than one bathroom in an Italian flat). It is not *immaculate* and not even *cac*, or central air-conditioning. The magic words are *grace* and *charm*, which have much the same effect on Europeans as a worm on a hook has on a fish.

As it turned out, the house actually did possess considerable grace and charm. The agent, Ms. Webb, had not lied. But even if she had, it would have been inadvisable to mention the fact because Patty Webb, a historian's wife, is slender, sprightly, and ever so sweetly autocratic. Her neatly trimmed gray hair and small face frame a pair of acutely observant eyes. She wears jeans. And she possesses the most stunningly effective bye-bye I have ever heard. After one of Patty Webb's bye-byes, there is simply nothing more to say.

She may be brisk, but that doesn't stop her being considerate. As well as taking our side in the negotiations with the owner, Patty intended to make sure we had a minimum survival kit. On the evening we moved in, she arrived with a pan, two plates, two forks, and two glasses that, in addition to the table lamp sitting on the floor, give the house a delightful day-after-the-Wall-Street-Crash look. If we had had a telephone, we could have ordered a pizza from Domino's, sat in the empty room, and toasted our arrival. That's what couples generally do in American films. We didn't have a phone so we went out for a hamburger instead. Locking the door behind us, we set off resolutely in the wrong direction.

. . .

FOR ITALIANS COMING to live in the United States, the greatest satisfaction derives not from seeing films six months before they are released in Italy, or choosing from fifty different kinds of breakfast cereal, or reading two kilos of newspaper on a Sunday morning. What really tickles our epiglottis is grappling with American bureaucracy. Why is that? It's because, having trained on the Italian version, we feel like a matador faced with a milk cow. It's a pushover.

Unfortunately, the experience doesn't last long and leaves you with a vague feeling of dissatisfaction. After sorting everything out, an Italian has a craving for a few more phone calls to make, some last-minute problem to unravel, or another clerk to convince. But it's no use. Americans see no existential significance

13

in, say, getting a phone installed (the struggle, the pleading, the long wait, the final victory). As soon as your new phone's dialing tone tells you it's connected up, they abandon you to your fate.

What now follows is the story of one short but exciting morning in action against the bureaucratic legions of Washington. Battle stations was a phone booth at Sugar's, a Korean coffee shop on the corner of P and Thirty-fifth streets. Weapons and ammunition—five quarters, paper, pen, passport, map of the city, a good command of English, and a moderate degree of optimism.

The first thing, in a country where everything is done over the phone, was to get a telephone. All this took was a call to C&P (the local—private and therefore efficient—equivalent of the Italian Telecom) to ask for a number. The clerk asked a few questions of the kind that any student on a beginner's English language course could answer—name, surname, age, address. At the end of the conversation, the same clerk told me, "Get your pen and write. This is your number. You'll be connected in twenty-four hours." Total time required for the transaction—ten minutes. Cost—twenty-five cents.

At this point, it is necessary to connect your new phone to a long-distance carrier. Competition among AT&T, MCI, and Sprint is ruthless. Each provider offers special conditions, such as discounts on numbers you call frequently, on calls to a foreign country of your choice, at particular times of day or on certain days of the week. Time required to decide—fifteen minutes. Cost—nothing. Each company has its own free phone number (which in the USA begin with 1-800).

Next came connection to cable television (one phone call to Cablevision, who specify the precise time at which their technicians will call the following morning) and insuring the contents of the house against theft or fire (ten minutes, no formalities). But to apply for a Social Security number, which is the de facto equivalent in the United States of an identity card, the phone is not enough. You need to go to the appropriate office, where a clerk asks you questions and types your answers straight into a computer. Queue (sorry, line)—none. Forms—ditto. Interview time—five minutes.

Then we made a visit to the police for a temporary parking permit. (Time—fifteen minutes. Cost—nothing.) After which to open a bank account, all you need to do is turn up with the money (essential), and proof of domicile. The address on a letter is okay. A photocopy of your rent contract is even better. A temporary checkbook is issued on the spot and you can choose the definitive version from a catalog. There's the classic model, the old-fashioned type, and one with Sylvester the cartoon cat on every check. My wife, of course, insisted on Sylvester. That was perhaps the most trying moment of the entire morning.

• • •

WE CAME FROM Italy without moving house in the true sense of the word. We just brought eight trunks containing the absolute minimum—a few pieces of silverware so that we would have something to worry about when we weren't in, one or two paintings, and carpets to prove we're sophisticated Europeans, and some books, clothes, T-shirts, and sneakers identical to those on sale in the United States.

We didn't bring any mattresses because we thought we could buy them at a reasonable price in America. That is true, of course, but there is a snag. In the Washington area, sixty retailers compete for the lower backs of 4 million residents and while the residents know what they want, we didn't have the foggiest idea.

Thus it was that, following the directions in the Yellow Pages, we pulled up outside a place called Mattress Warehouse (12125 Rockville Pike, telephone 230-BEDS), whose advertisement claimed low, low prices and a big, big choice (or it may have been the other way round). Their shrewd sales assistants are seasoned veterans who have done the business thousands of times. They're used to convincing old ladies with lumbago, horizontally extended families, and majestic African-Americans too tall for any mortal couch. When an unwitting out-of-towner crosses the threshold, their faces light up.

Cast your minds back for a moment to *High Noon*. The stranger arrives and advances silently across the deserted but mattress-encumbered floor. A lone figure breaks away from the group of sales assistants. He smiles, and walks slowly toward the new arrival (this is all in slow-mo). The sales assistant knows that his adversary has no chance. The stranger, who is unused to the surreal silence of a vast expanse of variously upholstered bedding accessories, loses his nerve and goes for his gun. He misses. What he actually does is say "I want a mattress," which by now is fairly obvious. Guided tours of Washington rarely include the Rockville Pike Mattress Warehouse. The sales assistant smiles at this point, for he knows he can finish the stranger off whenever he wants, and then decides to have some fun.

Our executioner is called Skip. He's tall, burly, and has hair slicked back like Joe DiMaggio's. His eyes shine with the fire of the professional while his colleagues sit back and take note. It's clear that Skip intends to put on a show. He begins by explaining American mattress sizes: twin (normal), full (large), queen (huge), and king (gigantic). Then he points out that mattresses look the same but they actually have different springs, mechanisms, and prices (and names like King Koil Posture Bond Extraordinaire, Beautyrest World Class Conquest Pillowtop, Posturepedic Westport Cushion Firm). The only way to find the one that suits us, he says, is to try them. No sooner said than done. Skip throws himself onto a double bed and obliges me to do likewise. Then he bobbles, he wriggles and he squirms. My wife watches in silence.

Skip goes from bed to bed, bouncing contentedly like a child in a sixties TV commercial. In the end, we make our choice, or rather Skip makes it for us—two phosphorescent king-size mattresses with gargantuan metal frames. They were delivered the following day, and it would immediately become clear that they were too bulky to go up the spiral staircase of a modest Georgetown residence. On the phone, Skip keeps his cool. It's so often the case, he says. However, we can cut them in half. It'll be fifty dollars per mattress. We take all major credit cards.

• • •

WHEN YOU MOVE into an empty house, mattresses and silverware aren't enough. You need tables, dining chairs, and easy chairs. In fact, you need all those things that Americans take with them in rented U-Haul vans when they move from one state to another. The United States is actually a republic founded on relocation. The whole social order is based on one assumption: people move house. Presidents move out of the White House, workers go where the work is, and children leave home for college. There are awesome mechanisms in place to facilitate these operations.

On signing a rent contract in America, the new tenant knows he or she will find only a fitted kitchen and fitted closets. In our case, the former was microscopic, with electrical appliances from a "Happy Days" set (the oven was a Caloric De Luxe) but the fitted closets were cavernous. Americans call them walk-ins because that is precisely what you do. If you're looking for a jacket (or rather, vest), you've got to step in, switch the light on and stroll among the clothes hangers.

At this point, however, our house stopped being quite so typically American. It had none of those appliances that transform so many American homes into a sort of NASA Mission Control (the ice machines, the remote-control barbecues, the windows that darken electronically). The building at 1513 Thirty-fourth Street was modern enough around 1956 but has since respectfully declined all invitations to catch up with the cutting edge.

The bathrooms are cramped, with diabolical English-style washbasins. The showers poke out over the bathtubs, protected by yellowing curtains. The windows are those guillotine-like sash affairs that either refuse to open at any price or slither miserably shut without warning.

Each of the windows is equipped with long safety screws, known as window locks, so that they cannot be opened from the outside. Insurance companies recommend them and give you a discount if you fit them to your home but, in my humble opinion, they are the most idiotic security devices around. They do present an obstacle, but only for the owners of the home. Let's say, for example, that you want to attract the mail carrier's attention. To do so you will have to: a) find the appropriate key, which is inevitably in another room; b) rotate the long screw in a counterclockwise direction; c) remove said screw; and d) open the window, which the painters will have sealed shut when they were painting it. By the time you have completed the operation, the unwitting delivery operative will be at the far end of the street. The other option is to attract your quarry's attention without opening the window. So if, as you are touring the United States, you notice someone waving dementedly behind a closed window, you will know that they have window locks fitted.

American windows have another feature that generates anxiety in Europeans. There are no blinds or shutters worthy of the name. Curtains, if any, are only there as decoration. After a while, you get used to it, but for the first few days you feel as if you are living in the middle of the street. You think everyone is watching you. As you sit in front of the television, you wonder if you should wave at people going past.

It's difficult to get to sleep at night without blinds or shutters, and impossible not to wake up in the morning. There's no point in saying that's how the Americans like it (being of rugged pioneer stock, they refuse to lie abed when the sun is high in the sky). Instead, you've just got to cover the windows with dressing gowns, newspapers, and paper bags. Even then, sometimes the blackout is less than total. During our first, distressed days, we dug out the eyemasks the cabin staff had handed out on the flight over and with their help, drifted like astronauts into a state of artificial suspended animation.

• • •

AFTER A COUPLE of visits to furniture rental companies (an experience I recommend to anyone with a sense of humor), and after having decided not to buy (not worth it for just one year), we decided to attack on three different fronts to acquire the remainder of our requirements—loans, flea markets, and shopping malls.

The idea of a furniture loan comes from a very European (i.e., formally flawless but usually impractical) piece of reasoning, which is this—if Americans spend hundreds of dollars to keep their furniture in storage, why not offer some of it a temporary home with us for free? The only problem is finding the right

American, which however turned out to be much easier than we expected. A friend of some friends was the new owner of a large quantity of postmatrimonial furniture and a much smaller amount of divorcée flat space. Storing it with us would save her a hundred dollars a month.

After a few false starts (the woman in question had a tendency to forget either the address or the key of her warehouse), her furniture was loaded onto a truck. The handover ceremony took place one afternoon in the middle of April when three sofas, four tables, eight chairs, two armchairs, and a television set made their formal entrance into 1513 Thirty-fourth Street. The curious mix of styles—Regency, Shaker, Santa Fe sofas, and assorted funeral parlor chairs—might possibly have inspired Edgar Allan Poe to pen a footnote to *The Philosophy of Furniture* but we were quite satisfied. Scratch a traveler and you'll find a masochist underneath.

At this point, we still needed desks, side tables, lamps, and bedside tables and to buy them we headed toward the big open-air market a short walk away from our home. Every weekend, the huge car park on the corner of Thirty-fourth Street and Wisconsin Avenue is the scene of Washington's answer to Portobello Road in London. You find one or two interesting items, industrial quantities of junk, and a large number of Italians making comments in loud voices. There are two fundamental differences between Wisconsin Avenue and Portobello Road. First, Wisconsin's prices are generally lower, and second, the Americans are not selling off their distant past (partly because they haven't got one) but their equally fascinating recent history. At Wisconsin, I discovered there is a market for antique computers (any pre-1985 model); that copies of *Life* magazine from 1975 are sold ready-framed; that toys from 1960 cost upward of fifty dollars (if I had been more far-sighted as a child, I would have cataloged and stored everything I had for sale at Wisconsin Avenue).

But furniture is an exception to this rule. Americans can't afford (most) antique pieces so they prefer modern ones. Anything that is merely old is of no interest. A gentleman by the name of James—a trader from South Carolina who writes "Let's talk" next to every price and has the deplorable habit of hugging his customers—sold us a sturdy fifties coffee table for twenty dollars and two thirties mahogany bedside tables for forty. The desk chair (fifty dollars) is an impressive wooden swivel job worthy of Sam Spade in *The Maltese Falcon*.

Transport for our purchases is on hand, offered by a friend of James's who, for ten dollars, will give us a lift in her station wagon with the seats taken out. We take her up on it and, sitting on the bare metal, we bounce back home along Thirty-fourth Street. Now we've got a kitchen out of "Happy Days," borrowed furniture, and two bedside tables with "Let's talk" written on them. For everything else, it's the malls.

• • •

POTOMAC MILLS LIES half an hour's drive south of Washington along Interstate 95. It is a spectacularly large mall whose tentacles spread out across the fields of Virginia, attracting 14 million visitors each year. Many of the shops are factory outlets and the prices are a third lower than in the shops in town. It's immensely easy to get lost and absolutely impossible not to buy anything. After one hour, Europeans are enjoying themselves like spoiled children. After two hours, they are scooping things up like refugees from the former Soviet bloc. The teen gangs—vulnerable, aggressive, inexplicably bored kids—recognize us. Mall walkers, those fanatics who keep fit by walking back and forth through shopping centers, hate us because we're in the way. That's right. We're the ones with the huge parcels and no trolley.

We came here to buy sheets, pillows, and blankets. But the problem with Potomac Mills is that the sheets, pillows, and blankets are camouflaged among other, much more interesting items. You can't help getting distracted.

The sporting goods shops, which are as big as the hangars at Heathrow Airport, can satisfy any athletic desire, no matter how perverse. A visit to the huge Levi's factory outlet induces the commercial equivalent of Stendhal's syndrome, the neurosis that the artistic masterpieces of Florence and Venice provoke in the more naïve sort of tourist. In the immense stores that sell female underwear, the newcomer can begin to take stock of American sexuality, and suspect that something may be wrong with it. The famous, embonpoint-enhancing Wonderbra is in fact an optical illusion. The Victoria's Secret catalog—a sort of vade mecum for American adolescents—hints that it comes from London (but it was actually launched in Ohio by a Californian).

And stalking Americans around an IKEA store is an education in itself. IKEA stores in the United States are totally different from their European counterparts. At the Milan or Stockholm store, the customers are looking for middle-quality furniture at low prices and, to achieve that end, they are prepared to assemble it at home. In the United States, putting the furniture together is what people want to buy. Having the item in the house afterward is the price they must pay. Americans, in other words, enjoy the process. The end result is fundamentally boring. When they have obtained what they want (a coffee table or a rocket landing on the moon), they move on to something else.

One of the few exceptions to this do-it-yourself rule is the armchair. American armchairs are too complicated to take apart and put together again, and have little in common with their British or Italian cousins. The English word *armchair*—a mere chair with arms—throws light on the profoundly stoic nature of the British. In contrast, Italian armchairs are magnificent to look at but all too often they should be carrying the warning they have when they're on show at the Guggenheim—"Do not sit."

But things are different in the United States. For at least two hundred years, the national spirit has been expressed through its armchairs. After rocking-chairs (which made the restless American dream of being on the move while sitting still actually come true) there were easy chairs, patented in the mid-nineteenth century and immediately established as a rich source of moral dilemmas. In *The Confidence Man* (1857), Herman Melville describes the "Protean easy-chair," "a chair so all over bejointed, behinged, and bepadded that the most tormented conscience must, somehow and somewhere, find rest."

In the hundred and fifty or so years that have followed, the process has been taken to extremes. Modern easy chairs will gratify any whim of the human spirit, offering positions from the fetal to the horizontal. The most straightforward recliners feature a back that goes down as the footrest springs up, while top-of-the-line models look as if they could swallow a child whole. Their names have a frighteningly perverse fascination. La-Z-Boy is a veiled invitation to commit a cardinal sin. Strato-lounger is more appropriate for an intercontinental bomber than a lounge chair and I can only imagine the legendary Bunkerlounger being used by a Nazi general, cyanide pill at the ready, and resplendent in black leather overcoat.

And the moral of the tale? For $143 (plus taxes), we purchased our recliner. Now every evening, like kids with a new garden swing, we quarrel over whose turn it is to use it.

May

*Y*ou don't go to America. You go back, even if it's only your first trip. Our brain is so full of American information that the country offers a never-ending sequence of déjà vu sensations. Every panorama looks as though you've already seen it. You feel as if everything you do, you've done before. America's sheer familiarity is unsettling. Only the noises sound as if they are really new. They're different, American noises.

It's a distinction you notice at night, in particular. The wood of the houses broadcasts a concert of creaks and groans that, taken together with the crime statistics, is more than a little disturbing. Anyone from Europe will need time to get used to it. For example, the reinforced concrete of Italian homes induces a crypt-like silence, which is heightened by the impenetrable darkness produced by shutters over the windows. America's not like that at all. Every night, in the bedrooms of this country, a kind of *son et lumière* show takes place. The yellow lights of the streetlamps shine in through the windows, punctuated by the glare of headlights.

The pipes, which are fitted externally onto the walls, emit sharp knocks and mysterious squeaking noises. And from this point of view, our house in Georgetown is particularly lively. The wood of the floors breathes. Bathrooms gargle. Windows thrum. Invisible avian visitors shriek like children and the crickets never shut up. Our neighbor, the allergy specialist, from whom only a thin wooden wall divides us, listens to classical music and dreams of new hypersensitivity disorders.

The day begins at six o'clock with the thump of the newspapers being hurled against the front door and the matutinal ablutions of a bird that has built its nest in the guttering about six feet away from our pillows. Half an hour later, a distant rumbling heralds the arrival of the first commuter cars on M Street. When one turns uphill into Georgetown along the uneven road surface, the rumbling intensifies, then fades away.

At seven o'clock on Tuesdays and Fridays, the clatter of the sanitation department truck approaches, to stop outside our door. At 7:02, we are regaled with the imprecations of the sanitation department operatives, who are dissatisfied with how our rubbish has been laid out (the rule is: glass and plastic—blue bag; household rubbish—black bag; paper—green box; leaves, grass cuttings and garden waste—that's our affair).

At seven-thirty, the room fills with the jingle of WAMU, a station affiliated to National Public Radio, which has the advantage of not broadcasting any commercials. Not that I have anything against advertising. It's just a question of timing. American advertising at eight o'clock in the morning—like fried fish—is nauseating. Italian commercials are a little easier to digest. Biscuits and diapers are promoted just before the radio news by the subdued voices of people who are aware that they are emerging from a radio alarm. Not by maniacs screaming out the discounts on today's special offers.

At nine o'clock, while I'm leafing through the papers, I hear the shouts of a group of children filing past the house from the nearby Montessori nursery toward the playground in Volta Park. There are twenty children in ten different colors. Every possible shade of hair and skin is represented. Naturally, none of them are looking where they're going. They jostle each other as they pass, laughing and looking anywhere but straight ahead. The accompanying teachers—one at the front and one at the back—wear the resigned air of cowboys who have ridden that particular trail many times before.

The passage of the small herd marks the beginning of the working day. From my desk, I note the other noises of the new morning. There's the pleasant chatter of the modem, which takes a little getting used to (at first I thought something was wrong with the computer and would stare at it apprehensively). Then comes the Armageddon-like crash of the toilets flushing next door. Airplanes fly low overhead on their way to the National Airport just across the river. On windy days, we can hear the ringing of the bells one of our neighbors has hung in his garden. It's an Alpine sound, which makes it vaguely surreal in Washington. The first time I heard the bell, I instinctively turned around to the window behind me expecting to see cows grazing under the magnolia and a shepherd in jacket and tie, like a Magritte painting.

As I sit at my desk, I can see the street through another two windows. About four yards of America traversed by students with loud voices and dogs out to do their worst to the flowerbeds. But the lords of the street are the joggers, to whom Thirty-fourth Street offers a challenge (on the way uphill) and relief (as they jog back down). The open window allows me to follow the rhythmic thump of sneakers on the sidewalk, the labored breathing of ruggedly built men, and the whimpers of women too exhausted to complain but too neurotic to stay at home.

Our street is a source of other everyday noises. Although narrow, Thirty-fourth Street is, together with Wisconsin Avenue, a thoroughfare that leads to the residential suburbs and the Potomac River. Every so often, the police and fire brigade speed along it, their lights flashing and their sirens at full blast. The lights and sirens are excessive and look as if they have come straight out of a child's imaginings (the real power of American police officers lies in the infantile panic they induce, I have often thought). The blue lights flashing back and forth on the roof, the red lights whirling behind, awesome screams, and an invisible loudspeaker that barks incomprehensible orders ("Pull over!" which means, "Draw over to the side of the road!" and not "Put on your jumper!"). Such special effects are not wasted on Italians. The only exception is a friend of ours. A few days ago, he waved down a police car and attempted to get in the back. He thought it was a taxi, or so he said.

Around midday, the letterbox begins to make quivering sounds, which means that the mail carrier has tried to insert something through the door. Every day, I thoughtfully get up to open the door for him. And every day when I get to the door the last letter has already been delivered. When I open the door, the postperson is already on his way to the next house. I've never seen his face, but I'd recognize his back anywhere.

When I'm working in a room, I rarely have the television on. In Russia and China, it was because I couldn't understand anything. I know other journalists who can work with CNN on, and secretly I admire them. Listening to the Cleveland correspondent interviewing a supermarket checkout girl for the fifth time is genuinely heroic. It's only at about two o'clock in the afternoon that I turn the TV on. (The set is a relic from the seventies. One American I know was moved to tears when he saw it. He said it reminded him of his childhood.) The jingle that introduces CNN news stimulates a pleasant Pavlovian response in me, drawing me into the basement kitchen where I have lunch with the refrigerator humming away behind me and a splendid view of strangers' socks passing in front of my face.

The real sound track for an American working day, however, is the ringing of the telephone and the purring of the fax machine. Phones in the States don't have that arrogant sound Italian ones make. They emit a gentle twitter, like some mysterious bird. At five in the afternoon, the usual fax from Milan arrives to a musical accompaniment. This is because the motorists backed up along Thirty-fourth Street have their radios on and their windows open. Their wait in front of my window lasts, on average, for one third of a song. When I manage to listen to one all the way through, it means either that M Street down on the corner is blocked or that three successive drivers have similar tastes in music and are tuned in to the same station.

Sometimes, instead of keeping my ears open and listening in on America, I watch the squirrels. I admit it might sound a curious way of passing the time but I would like to invoke in my defense the imagination of American squirrels. In this country, these little animals are spectacularly energetic. They climb up trees. They scamper down again. Then they clamber onto the roof, make a tremendous racket, rummage through the dustbins, and play hide-and-seek in the basil and the geraniums. One brown squirrel has acquired the habit of jumping onto the windowsill to see what I'm writing. This may indicate that American squirrels are not particularly discriminating, but it certainly also shows that Italian writers shouldn't be left alone for too long.

• • •

WE LASTED A total of exactly forty-four days without a car. Sometimes, on weekends, we would hire one, which is not a difficult operation. Whereas in Italy the clerk will look at you malevolently and fill out a form as long as a whole book of Virgil's *Aeneid*, all it takes in America is five minutes and a credit card.

We also got American licenses. Here's what you have to do. You go to the Division of Motor Vehicles, or DMV, and they give you a pink form with 103 questions and answers. (Not a round hundred. One hundred and three.) When you're ready, you sit at one of the computer terminals and take part in an exciting videogame of twenty questions. If you get fifteen right, you win. Your driving license, complete with photograph, will be handed over at once. There's one other thing—the questions are the same all day so, in theory, it's possible to organize team tactics (one candidate goes in and then tells friends and relatives). Italians, I have been able to note, are amazed at this demonstration of trust by the authorities. Often they are so shocked that they actually refrain from cheating.

Once you've got your license, you'll need to buy a car. This is your real initiation into American society. To do so, you have to go to the outskirts of the city to find a car dealer. In other words, if you want to buy a car, you'll have to rent one again. At the dealer's, the sales team is sitting in the reception area, vigilant as vultures. Like their colleagues in the mattress business, when they see a European, they let out a little whimper of pleasure. Actually, legend has it that car salespersons are shrewd and ruthless. One Italian diplomat confessed to me his technique for softening them up. He takes them to a bar and gets them drunk. A French lady I met at a friend's house told me she had bought a secondhand car, and had managed to drive it for a total of twenty-eight kilometers, or seventeen and a half miles. (She did, however, learn a new American word—lemon.)

Car purchase follows a precise ritual. The customer, having examined the vehicle, makes an offer and the salesman, who is playing the part of the good guy, goes into the office to talk to the dealer, or bad guy, returning with a yes or a no. The scene is repeated each time an offer is made. The negotiations take a disastrous turn when the salesman realizes that his victim cannot distinguish a Ford Mustang from a semitruck and is passionately in love with antiquated station wagons flaunting wood trim on the bodywork and names like Pontiac Parisienne. (Americans turn up their noses at them, and view them the same way Venetians look on gondolas. Strictly for the tourists.)

In preparation for our purchase, my wife and I had genned up on the various bargaining techniques with a manual we had bought specially (*The Complete Used Car Guide*). It was of absolutely no use whatsoever. In the huge Koons showroom at Tyson Corner, a salesperson called Rick and a manager in cowboy boots—who looked about sixteen years old—decided at once who was in charge. They were. We had made up our minds to buy a Japanese car, and not to spend more than five thousand dollars (*The Complete Used Car Guide*, page forty, "Figure your top price ahead of time"). When we left, we had an American car, and we had spent twice as much as we intended. Not only that. I think we were the first purchasers not to get a discount on the price advertised on the windscreen sticker. And we didn't even get one of the little mats that American used car dealers are so notoriously generous with when negotiations have been completed.

• • •

ANYWAY, WE CAME back to Washington in our car—a 1991 Ford Taurus with a leatherette interior. Getting it home was easy. Thanks to the automatic transmission, not even the most doggedly inept driver could have put it into second instead of fourth. But driving around town was more difficult than it seemed. Americans, while naturally prudent, do tend to extend their sense of ownership to the lane they are driving in, and won't give way for any reason at all. On the other hand, it is also true that they have a very democratic approach to junctions. You cross in strict order of arrival.

Driving along a freeway where everybody observes the speed limits—usually fifty-five miles, or ninety kilometers, an hour—is very relaxing, if slightly surreal. The cars look as if they are running on a conveyor belt. Many drivers use their cruise control, which blocks the accelerator at the speed limit and lets them get on with various ancillary activities. They eat, drink, change cassettes, read a road map, make phone calls, or indulge in a little shut-eye. The truly disturbing thing is that it is in these conditions, on the beltway that runs around Washington, that every so often there is a shoot-out. Driver A, proceeding at precisely fifty-five miles an hour, looses off a few rounds at driver B, who is guilty of doing no more than forty-five. Readers will understand that the imbeciles who throw stones from bridges over the *autostrada* in Italy look like pillars of society in comparison.

Then there's the problem of parking in town. The average American driver avoids the problem, if at all possible. It's not just for the cost. It's also because, being used to the vast parking lots of U.S. suburbia, he or she requires the equivalent of a medium-sized Italian town to maneuver in. But foreigners don't like parking in town in America, either, albeit for a different reason. That reason is the dreaded No Parking sign. Whereas in Italy a No Parking notice is little more than a statement of intent, in this country it is taken terribly seriously. No parking, in America, means that you can't park. The problem is to find out when. Here is what it says on one of the notices hanging on the lampposts on M Street:

> Tow Away No Standing
> Or Parking
> 7–9:30 a.m. 4–6:30 p.m.
> Mon.–Fri. No Parking
> Loading Zone 9:30–4 p.m.
> Mon.–Sun.
> One Hour Parking 9:30–4 p.m. Mon.–Sat.
> Tow Away No Parking
> 6:30 p.m. Fri.–4:00 a.m. Sat.
> 6:30 p.m. Sat.–4 a.m. Sun.
> If Towed 727-5000

"If towed"—on the last line—means "if they take your car away." As for the rest of it, if they had just written "Beat it," it would have been clearer and more honest.

For a month, we failed to understand anything and we got three fines a week. Then we decided to do what Americans do. They know that on any city street in the States where there are no parking meters they will find one of the following institutions: a) a car park around the back that you can't see from the road; b) a complimentary car park put at their disposal by the shop/office/cinema they are going to, provided they get their ticket stamped; c) valet parking. This means that an attendant, or valet, will take the keys to their car, hand over a token, and disappear with the vehicle.

The initial reaction of Italians to all this is: a) to park in the street anyway because "there aren't any *vigili* around anywhere" (they use the Italian term for local police, *vigili*, as if it were a universal category of the spirit); b) if they park in a covered lot, they forget to get their ticket stamped and block traffic on the way out while they argue with the attendant (and why call it *complimentary*? Wouldn't *free* have been simpler?); c) giving your car and keys to a young man in a car park is a question of trust, like handing over your luggage at an airport check-in desk. And everybody knows that Italians take nothing on trust.

• • •

ONE THING THE Pilgrim Fathers could never have imagined was that their descendants would triumph over fearsome enemies and gain world supremacy only to surrender before ten tiny adversaries, in various different combinations. It's not some mysterious form of bacteriological warfare. We're simply talking about the numbers from 0 to 9, which have ensnared the entire country like a spider's web. New arrivals, who already have plenty of numbers of their own, succumb in the space of a few weeks. Suddenly, that hateful tax code you left behind in Italy begins to look like an old friend.

Familiarity with numbers is a hallmark of all advanced societies, but in the United States figures have become the national sport. And foreign citizens have to take part in the game, whether they want to or not. Let's start with the date. The American habit of putting the month in front of the day is well-known but conceptually challenging nevertheless. To admit that 6-7-94 is the seventh of June and not the sixth of July is profoundly disquieting to many Italians, just as it would be if they discovered that the moon was actually cylindrical.

Then temperatures are measured in degrees Fahrenheit. If you want to know how many degrees centigrade (Celsius) it is, you have to take away thirty-two and calculate five-ninths of the figure you are left with. The operation is further complicated by the American custom of using expressions such as the low nineties (90–93°F = very hot) or the high teens (17–19° F = bitterly cold). In this case, to arrive at the centigrade equivalent you will have to tackle negative numbers, something you forgot how to do when you were thirteen. In fact, many of us never quite get used to all this. And discomfort degenerates into drama when you need to take someone's temperature. The legendary number thirty-seven—the watershed separating anxiety from peace of mind in Italy—means absolutely nothing to an American thermometer or medical practitioner. The news that "your little boy's temperature is a hundred and two" will hit the average Italian *mamma* like a sledgehammer, even though she wouldn't turn a hair at the equivalent 38.8 degrees expressed in Centigrade.

We'll draw a veil over the world of American gallons (different from British gallons), stones (equal to fourteen pounds), feet and inches (on my driving license it says 5-08: that's not my date of birth, it's how tall I am) and move on to other numbers. American streets go on forever—we bought our mattresses at 12125 Rockville Pike; one of our friends lives at 8123½—and are frequently called by a number. For example, Thirty-fourth Street runs right across Washington, disappearing and reappearing again like an underground river. House numbers are logical, but far from simple. Our own 1513 means that the building is near the junction with the road indicated by the fifteenth letter of the alphabet. Washington taxi drivers, who could get lost driving round their own backyard, do not seem to have grasped the concept.

The zip is ubiquitous. (It's not what we call a zip in Europe. It's an American postcode.) You get asked for it at the shops by market researchers. The short version has five figures (20007), otherwise there are nine (20007-2727). And a Social Security number is indispensable, even for those who are not entitled to the security American society offers. It's an identity document and you'll get asked for it in all sorts of circumstances (when you sign a check, when you're hiring a car). Admitting you haven't got one at dinner produces a bigger frisson of excitement than if you were to jump onto the table and start nibbling the hostess's ear.

But let's go on. Everybody has a driver's license number and several credit card numbers (with expiration dates, and two telephone numbers in case the card is lost or stolen—one to call in America and the other from abroad). Almost nobody has a telephone number—most people have two or three (phone, fax, modem) and the telephone companies give you a calling card, which also has a number. In some cases, this will be your phone number plus a personal identification number, the odious PIN. In other cases, though, the number will be completely different. The AT&T card, for example, has four numbers—domestic, international, PIN, and authorization code. AT&T also offers a prize scheme for subscribers (True Rewards) whose membership card has a number that is, obviously, different from all the others.

But we haven't finished yet. My e-mail address is a number. You need numbers and passwords to access databases from your computer. (You are given one automatically to start with—I got XALKEN-PURGE, which sounds like a Klingon swearword.) If you do a lot of traveling, it's worthwhile signing up for one of the frequent-flyer schemes. The number will be required when you book your flight and is added to the booking code. Every department store, supermarket, or car hire firm, from Macy's to Safeway to Hertz, has its own credit card (with numbers). Associations, bookshops, and gymnasia all offer membership, and yet more numbers. Without exception, all these numbers are printed on plastic cards, which you should in theory always carry with you. You can't, of course, unless you want to take a tip from your local bag person and push them around on a supermarket trolley.

Finally, there are the banks. Your account number will be printed on your checks next to the ABA (American Banking Association) code needed for bank transfers. ATM (Automatic Teller Machine) cards have another number printed on them, which in turn is different from the secret code number that "thou shalt not write down but shalt remember," as one of the Ten Contemporary Commandments enjoins. This is no small matter for anyone trying hard not to forget his Italian numbers (PIN code, suitcase combination lock, code to listen to recorded phone messages), particularly if you've only got one birthday and one wedding anniversary as memory joggers.

• • •

TRY TALKING TO any Italian who has lived in America. He or she will tell you that one of the few truly traumatic experiences is this. For American banks, what we are—and what we own—in Europe counts for nothing. This induces an uncomfortable feeling of having lost status, and one or two more concrete problems.

Consider the humble credit card. In America, to get a credit card you need a credit history. In other words, if you want credit, you've got to have debts. It's a well-known paradox, and one that non-Americans greet at first with open-mouthed incredulity, then quiet amusement, and finally with coronary-threatening fury. I can say with pride that from the middle of May on, I passed through every one of these stages.

The first phase—amazement—begins when the bank, after

opening your account and handing over your checks, declines to issue you with a credit card. Without one, everyday life in the USA is about as straightforward as climbing Mount Everest on a tricycle. Americans have been using credit cards since 1958 and couldn't live without them. (There are two hundred million Visa cards alone in circulation.) Putting it on plastic is one of the country's noblest traditions. Hiring a car is a good example. The alternative to a credit card is leaving a cash deposit. But cash deposits in the United States come just after drug trafficking in the suspicious activities stakes. They also pose problems, such as, where do you keep the cash? (A British friend told me that when he lived in America, he hid wads of dollars all round the house. Then he forgot where he'd put them.)

Stage two. The foreign visitor, his or her curiosity aroused by these customs, takes the applications, fills them out carefully—including the box that will prove fatal, "How long have you been living at your current address?"—and sends them off to Visa, American Express, and Mastercard. The refusals arrive on the same day. The respective companies, who are in cutthroat competition with one another and quite willing to issue a credit card to a concrete bollard, provided it's American, want nothing to do with us. The letters are identical, like the ones that would-be authors receive from publishers after sending unsolicited manuscripts. Sorry, you are an admirable person but the answer is no.

Foreign residents, who make it a perennial topic of conversation, know the reason for these refusals. Anyone who has just arrived has no credit history. In plain English, he or she has never asked to borrow money and is therefore adjudged not to be creditworthy. One of the refusals informed me that a credit reporting agency's credit scoring system had failed me on four counts: number of requests for credit (in other words, no debts); payments for housing (that is, no mortgage); residential status; and age. The letter went on to say that the Federal Equal Credit Opportunity Act forbids discrimination on the grounds of race, color, religion, national origin, sex, or marital status.

I try calling them. I admit that I am ashamed not to have contracted—in a whole month and a half—any debts or mortgages. I explain that because I was in Europe two months ago, I couldn't have been living at my present address. I humbly submit that at thirty-seven (ten years younger than the president), I think I'm old enough to be trusted with a credit card. But there is nothing doing. A young woman with a mellifluous voice informs me on behalf of American Express that a computer calculated my score, and computers don't listen to arguments. Of course, she solicitously concludes, if you had bought your car on installments, things would have been easier. But, unfortunately, I paid cash.

The third stage is anger. Determined to fight, I send off the applications again, explaining the absurdity of the situation and enclosing the proof (or rather, what I believe to be proof) of my sound financial standing—a letter from the Italian embassy, one from my employer, another from my bank in Italy, and a résumé that says that I am not a professional swindler.

Visa and American Express must have used them to make paper airplanes. Their replies were identical. Sorry, nothing doing. Finally, there was humiliation. The same companies that were refusing me filled newspapers, magazines, and restaurants with leaflets begging people to accept a credit card, using every insidious trick in the book. One card offered a Frequent Flyer mile for every dollar spent, another tempted the undecided with free tanks of gas, and a third saved up a percentage of what you spent as a down payment on a new car.

In the end, it was an English friend who told me how to get out of this Catch 22. Don't use the word *application*, he explained. Call American Express and say that you want to make a conversion of your Italian card. It worked. A few days later, I had my credit card and from then on I was inundated with offers for others (Plus Card, Gold Card, Platinum Card).

Indignant, I ignored them all.

June

$\mathcal{I}$ talians who take a good look round and realize that, yes, they are actually in America often fall victim to the Russian Tourist Syndrome. These are the symptoms—disorientation, an urge to buy everything you can lay your hands on, and the general impression of having disembarked somewhere in the future. It's not really a science-fiction kind of future. It's just, say, in five years' time, which is quite enough to put the most seasoned traveler off his or her stroke.

The shopping frenzy is nothing to worry about. It's endemic with Italians, and there's nothing you can do about it. What is slightly more embarrassing is the feeling that you don't know how modern life works. The tricks are simple enough, when you find out what to do, and any American kid will tell you all about them, probably with a hint of condescension, as if they were talking to a character out of "The Flintstones."

Here are one or two examples. The mail carrier arrives, hands over a package, and holds out a pen with no nib. The wrong thing to say is "This pen won't write." What you have to do is take it and sign the receipt on the liquid crystal display of a computer. Then there are American phones that cost next to nothing and do just about everything. They help you, they take you by the hand, they encourage you, and they tell you what to do (for information, press 1; to make an order, press 2; to speak to our representative, press 3; if you've still got a rotary-dial phone, you should be ashamed of yourself and wait).

Services like CompuServe, Prodigy, and America Online—which you access over the phone via modem—have become part of daily life. Millions of people every day get information and send e-mail messages while they are sitting at their desks. That doesn't mean that they feel like characters out of a science-fiction novel. And therein lies one of the many differences between Italy and the United States. We treat science and technology with a respectful detachment that masks our fundamental lack of interest in the subject. But Americans don't respect science. Depending on the historical context and the mood of the moment, they adore it, they abuse it, they talk about it, they fiddle with it, they laud it to the skies, or they damn it to hell. But they get to grips with it. They actually use science.

America's problem—and Italy's revenge—is that sometimes the system gets too sophisticated, and ends up becoming ridiculous. The electronic exchange of information over the Internet is sometimes more complicated, and less efficient, than a phone call. Multiple-choice telephones (press button 1; press button 2) may be available twenty-four hours a day but they are far from intelligent. They go through the whole shopping list every time and if what you want isn't there, then you're in trouble. The mail carrier may have a portable computer but he still leaves at our house the letters intended for Miss Margaret O'Connor, who lives in the house on the next street that has the same number.

The same goes for novelty gadgets, one of America's national passions. Any catalog whatsoever—and there are ten thousand of them in circulation—will demonstrate that just because it's electrical or electronic doesn't mean that an object isn't stupid, or worse, completely pointless. I would dearly like to know, for example, just who it was who invented the solar-powered air-conditioned golf cap, that monstrous caricature of the American dream—a sports article (golf cap) with all mod cons (air-conditioned) that is also environmentally correct (solar-powered).

So, there's the crux of the problem. You have to distinguish, in this tropical rain forest of supply, the necessary from the superfluous, the tool from the toy, and the service that will enhance your lifestyle from the contraption that will only serve to complicate it even further. It's a jungle out there in America, nowadays. The consumer is pitted against the promoters of consumption. The battle is waged over the phone (where you get the most amazing offers); by fax (the most basic model has a hundred-page manual); and on TV (as Bruce Springsteen put it, "Fifty-seven channels and nothing on"). The humblest PC can do thousands of different things, 80 percent of which are completely useless, and has enough memory to last 110 years should its owner decide to write a letter every day (I've worked this one out).

We Europeans are defenseless before this onslaught. Americans, as we have said, are much more familiar with technology, and it's not a recent thing. Thomas Jefferson, who wrote the Declaration of Independence, invented dozens of futuristic (for the time) devices. One of them was a wrist-mounted thingummy for writing with two pens at the same time (the first photocopier?) and a "travel desk" that, with a little goodwill, you could think of as a rudimentary computer. Monticello, Jefferson's residence in Virginia, is an astounding museum of gadgets and proof of America's inventiveness. There have always been two guiding principles. Make it small and make it portable. "The man who changed the face of America," a magazine wrote a few years ago, "had a gizmo, a gadget, a gimmick—in his hand, in his back pocket, across the saddle, on his hip, in the trailer, round his neck, on his head, deep in a hardened silo. The typical American way of improving the human situation has been by means of crafty and usually compact little packages."

But not all inventors had Jefferson's imagination, or his freedom of action. In the last two hundred years, lots of things have been invented. The Nation of Little Packages, in other words, has not changed—but now sometimes it doesn't know what to do with those little packages. The list of useless things I have risked buying over the last few months would be lengthy. I will restrict myself to mentioning several varieties of palm-sized computers that you program with a pen. Then one day I realized that these gizmos weigh rather more than a notepad and are a lot more expensive.

. . .

PERHAPS IF YOU live in a log cabin in Montana, electronic shopping will change your life. But for anyone who lives near a shopping mall—roughly 90 percent of the population of the United States, for example—it's easier to pop out to the store yourself. I say this with a certain regret. I would be very happy to be able to put on a shirt I had bought by computer but it would probably be too long in the sleeve and not quite the right shade. Still, it would be a good way of breaking the ice at parties.

If anyone is actually interested in the details of my sartorial debacle, here is a blow-by-blow account. I accessed Compu-Serve. A display with twelve symbols appeared on the screen. These included an airplane (travel), a banknote (investments), a book (information), and a supermarket cart (shopping). Obviously, to buy a shirt you ignore the book and the aircraft and head straight for the fourth symbol. Click. The computer welcomes me to a place called an Electronic Mall, and asks me how I want to proceed—by article, by brand, by company, or by shop. I select "shops" and a list of names comes up, including Brooks Brothers, who make the excellent English-style shirts that we Italians have always liked to buy in America.

Things are getting exciting. I'm in the terminal emulator now, so I can type instructions on my keyboard instead of clicking on icons. Then all of a sudden, the computer invites me to take part in a quiz game. There's a prize draw for a $75 gift voucher for all those who can guess "who wore a Brooks Brothers shirt at the Yalta conference." I'm tempted to answer "Stalin," but I quash the impulse. My objective is to buy a shirt, not to broaden my historical horizons.

My electronic interlocutor, disappointed at my lack of competitive spirit, offers me three options—sportswear, womenswear, and business attire. I choose the last of these. A new menu then appears—complete wardrobe, jackets, trousers, classic shirts, or ties. I tap in number four, for classic shirts. At this point, a spectacular panegyric lauding Brooks Brothers shirts appears on the screen. It tells me they have collars with hand-stitched buttons that give them their characteristic roll, longer tails so you can tuck the shirt more firmly into your pants, and seven buttons on the front to keep the shape and relieve the distance between the buttons. For an extra charge, I can order a monogram with my initials.

I carry on. The next menu offers nine kinds of shirt, going from the majestic Brooks Finest Broadcloth Button-Down Collar ($95) to a Blended Dress Shirt ($38) which sounds very much like a cotton mix. I choose number four, 100% Cotton Pima Oxford Button-Down Collar ($48). The computer begins to bombard me with questions. How many? What color? What neck size? What sleeve length? Do I want a monogram? What initials? What color do I want the monogram? Where do I want it? I can feel my fingers tensing. I realize that if I hit the wrong key, I'm going to find myself with ten shirts the size of donkey jackets and I won't even be able to blame it on the sales assistant. I chicken out and hit the exit icon. The computer informs me that my order for a blue shirt, size 15½ 100% Cotton Pima Oxford Button-Down Collar (no monogram) has been canceled. A green glow emanates from the screen, as if in rebuke. But it might just be my imagination.

. . .

THE IMPRESSION I have described—an Italian arrives in the United States and gets the feeling that he or she has been living in the Stone Age—doesn't last for very long. For three months, you listen in awe as everyone talks about virtual reality and on-line friends. Then the doubts begin to emerge. How many people have actually bought an airline ticket by computer instead of phoning their travel agent? How many have ever sent data electronically and how many continue to use their fax? How many have ever spent an evening chatting to four strangers over the Internet? And even more important, who made them do it? Cyberspace (the name invented by a young science-fiction writer ten or so years ago) is a territory that it is worth getting to know. But there's also a risk it will turn out to be one of the following—a waste of time, a cop-out from real life, or yet another way of complicating simple operations.

What's all the fuss about, then? It comes from a combination of two reactions—excitement (something really important's happening!) and anxiety (oh my God! I'm going to get left behind!).

Teenagers behave like adults (they don't waste their time philosophizing about computers—they use them) and we grown-ups carry on like youngsters. Being able to learn something new is too good to be true, so we go at it with an enthusiasm matched only by our lack of discrimination. I know of one university professor who logs into various on-line discussion groups in the evening and pretends to be a (black) Labrador.

This enthusiasm will, I am certain, be followed by a sense of partial disappointment. It has already been the case with other inventions that were hailed as revolutionary but didn't actually change very much. Take interactive television (people can live without working in the evening as well just when they have finally managed to collapse onto the couch). Or the video-telephone (probably consigned to the dustbin of history by women: Do you really want to have to check your makeup just to answer the phone?). Or those versatile household robots that fired our youthful imaginations. All have gone straight from being science fiction to yesterday's news, and no one mentions them anymore.

Finally, it is interesting to note how Americans have favored some forms of technology and rejected others. Mobile phones, for example, are quite popular in the United States but nothing like as ubiquitous as in Italy. Video entryphones have failed to make a significant impact (Americans would rather have a gun in their house than a screen on the street). And what about car radios, which were invented in America (Motorola, 1928)? A model that tells you the name of the station was launched here as a revolutionary breakthrough the other day. In the suburbs of Milan and Naples, juvenile delinquents wouldn't even consider stealing a car radio that didn't have that feature.

• • •

FOR PEOPLE FROM Italy, America is one big party. The World Cup is about to begin and this gives us a rare opportunity. We can be experts. The United States has very little idea about soccer but right now everyone feels it is their duty to find out more. Having watched hours of baseball in uncomprehending silence, it is time to get my own back.

The title of expert is handed out with easy generosity. You don't actually have to prove your qualifications, which is just as well in the case of many expatriates. You don't even need to show your passport. A decent accent will do. Anyone who can pronounce the word *soccer* with a European accent is automatically an authority on the subject. You can now begin to make forecasts on who is going to win, criticize children kicking a ball around on the grass, and pour scorn on the level of warm-up tournaments, where footballers who would be booed off the field at a parish match in Lombardy turn out for the crowds.

No one is going to object. When an Italian talks about soccer, America listens. And not out of politeness. People are genuinely interested and spectacularly uninformed. All you need to amaze your audience for half an hour is to have watched the occasional Sunday evening soccer roundup in Italy, or perhaps to have collected half an album's worth of Panini soccer star cards.

Anyone can be a soccer pundit. Even those, like me, who have only a modest knowledge of the game. All the residents of Thirty-fourth Street are familiar with my views on the role of soccer in Italian cinema. My humble efforts in amateur soccer in Italy (*Terza Categoria* translates beautifully into an impressive Third Category) enabled me to entrance a woman from New York at dinner one evening. By the end of our conversation, she had fallen in love with the word *parastinco*, which means shinguard. She told me it sounded like a kind of Ancient Greek infantryman.

• • •

THE FIFTEENTH WORLD Cup is the result of a misunderstanding. It's not a soccer competition, as we have been led to believe. It's a crusade that intends to convert the infidel, by fair means or foul, including sponsor-inspired, hard-sell techniques, the excitable allure of Italian fans, and the serious, competent commitment of German players. If by next month we have managed to initiate Americans into the mystical joys of a round football hitting the back of the net, we'll have done it. Otherwise, they'll have won, as usual.

The nomination of the United States as World Cup host nation can only be explained in terms of this missionary spirit. If not, we would be forced to conclude that it was an act of madness, like organizing the World Series in Corsica or deciding to hold the next Superbowl in the Ukraine. There's no tradition, no interest, and there isn't even a proper name for the game because the word *football* has been hijacked by those overmuscled gentlemen with the padded shoulders. What America does have is sports facilities, money, a superb communications infrastructure, and above all limitless goodwill. Americans are impeccably well-mannered. They've got to host the World Cup so they'll try to like soccer. The spectacle is magnificent and moving at the same time.

The reasons why Americans are unenthusiastic about soccer have been endlessly debated all over the world but in the last few weeks discussions have acquired the flavor of a philosophical controversy. Some have maintained that the problem with soccer is that not enough happens. The players don't score enough points (unlike basketball), don't play enough innings (unlike baseball), and don't engage in enough physical violence (unlike football and hockey). One commentator put it in sexual terms, calling soccer "endless, delightful foreplay." Another compared a game of soccer to the ballet *Swan Lake*, perhaps not the entertainment of choice for a trucker from Kansas.

Over the last month, just about everything possible has been done to persuade Americans that it is their patriotic duty to enjoy the occasion. Newspapers have published soccer guides in installment form with lavish illustrations and diagrams, most of which are incomprehensible to those who do know the game. The *New York Times* explained the advantages of the goalkeeper coming off his line by calculating the angles (the keeper had so many lines extending from his body he resembled a Leonardo Da Vinci figure). It illustrated the various stages of the overhead, or bicycle kick, including falling onto a stiff arm that looked likely to guarantee a sprain. It pointed out that to get the ball past a wall of defenders you had to pull off one of the famous banana kicks (in the bars of Italy, *il calcio a banana* is renowned as the trademark of certain unlamented AC Milan center-forwards of the past).

When Americans take a serious interest in soccer—and many are doing so with a determined courtesy that honors their nation—they demand logical answers. But it is no coincidence that the best teams come from some of the most irresistibly irrational nations on earth—Brazilians, Argentines, and Italians. (There are the Germans too, of course, but they manage to do everything well.) How a game will end, and how a team or a player will behave, are completely unpredictable. Camus wrote of soccer that "I learned that the ball never goes where you think it will. This has helped me in life."

But try telling that to the Americans. It's just not possible, and they'll also want to know what position Camus played (goalkeeper). The average American approaches soccer like a pathologist: he (or she) cuts it open to find out what's inside. Facts.

Numbers. Statistics. You can't simply say that the other team was incredibly lucky and the refereeing was scandalous (these are concepts that translate into any language). Oh no. America demands that victories and defeats should have a justification. Soccer, like everything else, has to be scientific. Whether the science is physics, physiology, statistics, tactics, psychology, or meteorology is immaterial. The vital thing is to have an explanation that doesn't depend on good luck or the moral rectitude of the referee.

• • •

THIS MINUET OF alien cultures is as fascinating a spectacle as the finest game of soccer. On the one hand are the soccer tourists, the Hispanic minority, soccer-playing youngsters, and resident foreigners. On the other is the great American public, anxious to understand what is so enthralling about a nil-all draw. Experts urge them on, offer examples and make suggestions ("You say there aren't many goals in soccer? Then make every goal worth six points, like American football"). Ordinary Americans turn up their noses, pick at what's in front of them, and play for time, like 200 million preteens faced with an unfamiliar dinner menu.

The problem, they maintain, is that soccer and television just don't mix. To prove it, they resort to magnificently abstruse explanations. Some will tell you that the soccer field is too big and there are too few players, which creates a sort of televisual agoraphobia. Others complain at the lack of action. Ninety minutes spent waiting to see three corners by Bolivia is not the average American's idea of a good time. There's also a vocal lobby in favor of advertising, which claims that American attention spans, food intakes, and prostate problems require frequent commercial breaks. Forty-five minutes without hitting the remote (it's known as surfing here), rummaging through the refrigerator, or paying a visit to the bathroom could be life-threatening if repeated too often.

The other difficulty is this. Americans love the innocence of a kick-around in the countryside, not the hysterical, win-at-all-costs soccer of TV. They want a game without heroes that they can play as well as watch. Often, they do so in mixed-sex teams. They appreciate the physical effort required and the modest cost involved (it was the lower insurance premiums that convinced American schools to switch from football to soccer). Every weekend, the parks are full of junior All-American soccer players, both male and female, cheered on by eager parents who can't distinguish a crossbar from a corner flag. A sport that requires nothing more complicated than a few shirts and a field looks like the perfect solution for a land that loves to keep things simple.

So why hasn't soccer managed to catch on? It's because it has come up against the combined forces of the traditional U.S. sports, which at various times of the year trigger Pavlovian reactions in the minds of most Americans. The crack of the bat provides the sound track for summer. During the fall, Sunday afternoons and Monday evenings are occupied by the solemn rituals of American football. Winter and spring bring with them the thump of the basketball against the backboard, the deafening, rhythmic chants of the fans, and the rantings of the commentators. These noises, and these colors, produce violent reactions in the American psyche—a thirst for ice-cold beer to be imbibed at a favorite bar and a desire for pizza in front of the television set.

This is what soccer, so beloved of young children and immigrants, is up against. When the children are older, and the new arrivals have settled in, then perhaps soccer will have a slightly better chance.

July

*S*ummer in the United States is not a matter of calendar, custom, or climate. It's a question of air-conditioning. The change of season is announced by the thrumming of the first HVAC installation restarting and the complaints of the first Italian, who was too hot before and is too cold now. At that precise moment, summer has officially come to the United States.

We—it has to be admitted—were ready. For three months, friends and acquaintances had been warning us—Washington summers are dreadful. Flowers wilt. The sky looms. New arrivals have difficulty breathing. Until not so very long ago, Washington was actually classified by diplomats as a hardship posting. In the thirties, precise regulations laid down that as soon as the thermometer reached 95° Fahrenheit (35° Celsius), federal employees should be sent home. At the end of June, the *Washington Post* published an article about a family with no air-conditioning, as if they were a troop of endangered monkeys.

These admonitions elicited only smiles on our part. Friends—we replied—we grew up in the Po valley. We can take anything.

Almost anything, we should have said. We certainly weren't prepared for Washington summers. After two hours in an environment that we find unbearable and our neighbors disingenuously call warm, we are wandering round the house in search of the air-conditioning switch. At the first sign of difficulty, I decide to call a number printed on the label stuck on the compressor. It is the first time in my life that I have called a number on a label, which should give you some idea of how desperate I am.

Thanks to the advice offered by a technician over the hotline—and never was a name more appropriate—our ancient air-conditioning unit slowly heaved into action. Thus was initiated a long, tormented relationship between Italian tenants and indigenous climate control apparatus, mediated by a thermostat whose mode of operation was and remains a mystery. Actually, we were grateful for the thermostat but we were also totally at its mercy. To find out whether the air-conditioning was working, we would run to the window and look to see if the greenery that disguises the horrendous parallelepiped of the compressor was shaking violently, as if invested by a Mediterranean squall. If it was, the air-conditioning would be working, so we could begin to complain.

Over the first fifteen days of July, we came to understand many things. The first of these was that in America, air-conditioning in summer, like central heating in winter, is brutal. The equivalent devices in Italy may show a certain restraint, as if they are embarrassed to alter the pattern of the seasons, but American air-conditioning systems are unashamedly efficient. Hot here does not mean tepid. It means searing. And cold has nothing to do with merely chilly. We're talking arctic. Americans who go into an office, or a theater, or a museum, are looking for a violent shock, not a caress. For those in search of extreme experiences in Washington, I would propose: the National Air and Space Museum;

Dahlgren Chapel at Georgetown University; and the Safeway supermarket on Wisconsin Avenue, where the goose bumps on the customers provide an attractive counterpoint to those on sale in the poultry section.

Nonetheless, criticism is an expression of interest. Air-conditioning is by now an obsession. Before the end of July, I am able to debate the topic with a professor of physics, a historian, and a refrigeration technician. It is my favorite theme of conversation at dinner parties. In fact, I am sure people actually avoid sitting next to me so as not to be subjected to the following little dissertation.

• • •

A RUDIMENTARY VERSION of air-conditioning was introduced in 1881 (in the month of July, of course) to cool the room where the president, James Garfield, lay mortally wounded after being attacked by a lunatic. The air from outside was introduced into the room through a mass of ice and so—more or less—chilled. The invention of modern air-conditioning is attributed to Willis Carrier, who in 1902 installed a unit in a Brooklyn printing works. At first, it was just a piece of apparatus to treat indoor air because the name "air-conditioning" was only proposed by Stuart W. Cramer four years later.

Here in Washington, the House of Representatives had air-conditioning installed in 1928, the Senate in 1929, and the White House in 1930. In the fifties, thanks to AC—I'm using the acronym to show just how familiar I am with the subject—productivity in government offices in the capital rose by 10 percent. The first window-mounted model dates from 1951, and sparked off the air-conditioning boom in private homes. Today, Americans spend $25 billion every year on electricity for air-conditioning units.

When I'm not stunning those present with a barrage of statistics, historical facts, and technical data, I philosophize. Your urge to control the outside world (from Bosnia to Korea, to death and the weather)—I explain to any Americans who are willing to listen—is well-known and widely admired. It is the antithesis of passive resignation and has spurred the United States to the achievements we all know about. In America, air-conditioning is not simply a way of cooling down a room. It is an affirmation of supremacy. You Americans—I conclude with a professorial mien—nurture an instinctive diffidence toward fresh air. In your eyes, it is suspiciously anarchic.

There is a sound basis for this theory. In our basement, where the kitchen and dining room are located, the windows are sealed by at least five coats of paint. According to the worker who came to prize them open, they hadn't let in air from the street for forty years. The "nineties," less forty, makes "fifties." In other words, our windows hadn't been opened since air-conditioning made its triumphal entrance into the private homes of Washington. When Henry Miller wrote *The Air-conditioned Nightmare* in 1945, he evidently knew what he was doing.

. . .

AMERICAN BATHROOMS ARE usually commodious. Not only that. They reveal a love of personal cleanliness that verges on the obsessional. In the United States, the bidet is not rejected out of pique, as it is in Great Britain, for its absence is (partially) justified by the number of showers people take each day. In the United

Kingdom, showers are essentially a meteorological phenomenon. In America, they have been transformed into a mystic experience. Motel chains compete to see who can install the highest-pressure sprays, which now resemble the water cannon that police forces use to disperse particularly tenacious demonstrators. Once you have recovered from the initial shock, a brisk shower can be seen as a laudable American custom that foreigners adopt gladly. And that's why, at 1513 Thirty-fourth Street, we're getting worried. For the past two weeks, the second-floor shower (it would be on the first floor in Italy) hasn't been working properly. Water emerges, but without the customary brio. We call Patty Webb, our agent and substitute mother. She lends a sympathetic ear and promises to send some of her trusted plumbers. We ask her why she uses the plural. One averagely proficient plumber ought to be sufficient to restore our shower to its original ferocious efficiency. Patty says, "You'll see."

The plumbers—two of them, as promised—arrive the following day. Their names are John Marx and Joe DiMeglio, and they are no spring chickens. Let's just say that they have reached that indefinable age that, in the USA, brings with it special discounts and holidays in Florida. Marx and DiMeglio, whose life histories are complicated and whose phone numbers are known only to the Secret Service, are untypical of American workmen. They approach their job with an air of vague superiority. Having spent sixty years looking at faulty showers, they aren't going to let ours throw them.

Marx, we note, is particularly self-assured. He uses our phone, sprawls in the bedroom easy chair, sips Coca-Cola, peers into the boiler, and drifts off to sleep. He teeters perilously on the edge of the bath and asks us to hold him steady. But he's a master of his craft. "You want a more powerful jet?" he inquires, proving that he understands perfectly what he has been pretending not to know for the past hour. "You need an illegal showerhead." "Illegal? Why?" "Because," he explains with the air of a teacher addressing one of his least promising students, "the new energy-saving regulations require small holes, and small holes make the shower weak." "You want a strong shower?" he concludes. "Fit an old showerhead. Twelve dollars. I'll bring it round tomorrow."

Marx came back the next day, with the old-style showerhead. He was right, of course. A violent jet of water immediately sprang from the shower. Marx looked on in satisfaction. "Tell me the truth, Italian. You don't like it because it's strong. You like it because it's illegal."

. . .

IN THEIR STRUGGLE against the Great Enemy (the weather in any shape or form), Americans not only make use of air-conditioning and frequent, bone-shattering showers. They have other weapons. Or rather, they have a whole arsenal of them.

The most sophisticated weapon is explanation. We've already seen this in connection with sport. To explain a phenomenon, in the eyes of a fundamentally rational nation, is one way of defusing its explosive—and subversive—charge. The weather is therefore subjected to maniacally detailed analysis. The attitude has nothing whatsoever to do with the British passion for the same topic. In stoical Albion, talking about the weather is a way of looking forward to the discomforts it will bring. In the logical United States, it's a damage-limitation strategy.

There's always a note of alarm in American weather forecasts. TV weatherpeople have glassily inexpressive eyes. Even when they're making one of their little jokes, they give the impression that they're keeping back some tragic piece of news. There's an entire channel (the Weather Channel) that deals exclusively with the subject. In fact, it ferrets out disasters in every corner of the Union. Hurricanes, floods, storms, downpours, eclipses, land-slides—any calamity will do. It's the meteorological version of a horror film, and we foreigners are unaccustomed to the concept.

The local broadcasters, naturally, take no notice and continue to serve up a concentrate of bad news. This sadism can reach as-tounding heights of sophistication. During the summer, it is not sufficient to communicate infernal temperatures. There's also a comfort index, calculated from the combination of heat and hu-midity. And winter is not just a question of bitter cold. There is also the windchill factor, a temperature that takes wind-speed, and the consequent sensation of increased cold, into account. The phenomenon is well-known in Alpine valleys but the Amer-icans have classified it and turned it into a science.

Knowing the exact quantity of discomfort—being able to say exactly how badly you feel and why—is the first step toward the goal of every U.S. citizen: to feel good. We've mentioned the lav-ish use of air-conditioning. The importance of showering—in a country convinced that natural body odor is identical to the smell of shower gel—cannot be overestimated. But now I would like to talk about another of the weapons that are essential in the battle against summer. Ice.

For Americans, ice is an old friend. The term *icebox* (the fore-runner of the refrigerator) dates back to 1839, and in the subse-quent decades, millions of tons of its principal component served to alleviate the country's atrocious summers. Frozen white wine, fruit juice that chills the stomach, and iced beer (literally—you have to wait until it thaws before you can drink it) with names like Arctic Ice, which are advertised against images of glaciers and av-alanches. These are experiences that every new arrival knows—and fears.

The European terror of America's ice is not a recent phenomenon. In *Brideshead Revisited*, Evelyn Waugh demonstrates that in the thirties, British visitors had to fend off such attacks. Halfway through the book, the hero is on board a transatlantic liner leaving New York, and a steward comes up to him.

"Can I get you anything, sir?"
"A whisky and soda, not iced."
"I'm sorry, sir, all the soda is iced."
"Is the water iced, too?"
"Oh yes, sir."
"Well, it doesn't matter."

He trotted off, puzzled, soundless in the pervading hum . . .
The steward returned with whisky and two jugs, one of iced
water, the other of boiling water; I mixed them to the right
temperature. He watched and said, "I'll remember that's
how you take it, sir."

After three months in the United States, I have been able to confirm that nothing has changed. I don't drink whisky (or whiskey), so my lack of comprehension becomes clear on other occasions. For example, I am still not used to the quantity of ice that is served with soft drinks. Every time, I swear I will get in first but bartenders are always too quick for me. When I hear the ominous sound of ice rattling into the glass, I know it's too late. At this point, there are only two options, neither of them pleasant. Either you gulp down your drink, anesthetizing your gullet, or you wait until the cubes have melted, and then ingest the ensuing sticky mess.

But the bane of all Italians is the ritual of the glass of ice-filled water placed on the table of restaurants, cafes, and pizzerias everywhere as soon as the customer sits down. Some visitors, noting that the service is complimentary, think it is a delightfully courteous American custom. Most Italians, however, correctly perceive the imposition of this glass of iced water as a form of violence. And wasn't the water torture one of those fiendish medieval punishments?

This is how the modern version works. You go in. A young waiter (usually the one at the bottom of the pecking order) sneaks up behind you and pounces, thrusting a bucket full of ice and water onto your table. Let's say you manage to persuade your tormentor to take the offending item away. A minute later a second bucket bearer will try again (refusing to believe that a customer doesn't want a free drink). You repulse him as well. Two minutes later the head waiter will notice that yours is the only table in the restaurant without a bucket of iced water. Convinced that you are being deprived of something you are entitled to, he sorts out the problem personally. Head bowed, you accept defeat. You don't drink any, of course—that would be to risk a devastating attack of colitis. But you resign yourself to thinking of it as an insurance policy. After all, you'll be left alone now.

• • •

A FEW EVENINGS ago in a restaurant near M Street, I realized there was something odd about the atmosphere. It wasn't the usual uproar of young people having a celebratory meal out. Nor was it the familiar smell of French fries. This was something completely new. I thought about it all evening and concluded that it was the waiter. He was behaving strangely. Instead of aggressively informing us of his name and telling us the story of his life, he introduced himself with a curt "Good evening." He was relaxed, professional, and very dignified. Toward the end of the meal, I had to ask him, "Excuse me, where are you from?" "Italy," he told me.

That was when things fell into place. I was happy not so much because I had met a well-mannered compatriot as because, for once, I had avoided the company of America's hyperactive restaurant staff. It was gratifying—I must admit—to have given the evening's Chuck the slip, and not had to listen to a full blast, "Hi, folks. My name's Chuck!" as he handed me the menu (his name would of course be clearly printed on his badge). Serving the first course, Chuck would have told me he came from Indiana. The second course would have been accompanied by his educational background. And with the dessert he would have told me that he didn't have a girlfriend.

Now please don't misunderstand me. Americans are wonderful people. The problem, perhaps, is that they don't always realize that customers sitting at table in a restaurant might not want to meet yet another wonderful person. They may possibly want to know whether that exotic name on the menu is just another alias for the usual chicken. This is not hardness of heart. It's merely wanting to be left in peace. When bright young Brenda bounces up to ask you for the fourth time if everything is okay, there is an overwhelming urge to answer that, yes, everything would be fine if she stayed at the cash desk and chatted to her friends about films and boyfriends. Unfortunately, it's not physically possible. Brenda makes sure you have your mouth full before she asks you, "Is everything okay?"

American restaurant staff simply do not understand these things. They are the Red Guards of Good Intentions, always on the lookout for someone to make happy, and the part-time staff—often students at the local university—are by far the worst. An overliteral interpretation of the word *waiter* might induce you to construe it as someone who waits. Certainly, nothing upsets the digestion like a Georgetown freshman counting how many mouthfuls of your hamburger are left before swooping from behind to whisk away your plate.

The subject is a meaty one and the crucial point is your interpretation of the word *service*. For many people in Europe, serving is dishonorable (it's nothing of the sort, of course), while too many Americans think of it as a competitive sport. If I hadn't realized this, I might think that the sturdily built young woman sitting on my table—not at my table but actually on it—was being rude. Of course, she isn't. She just thinks that's the way to be friendly and earn her 15 percent tip, and my terrorized expression isn't going to change her mind.

Ah, the tip. At this point in the evening, the noisy courtesy that accompanied the meal is transmuted into a silent diffidence. The waiter is seized by a terrible uncertainty. The foreign customer might not be aware of the American tipping ritual, which lays down that the service charge should be at least twice the local taxes (if your waiter doesn't think you can be trusted, he or she will add service directly to the bill). For Italians, who are used to getting away with a few thousand lire at home, leaving 15 or 20 percent of the bill as a tip is yet another psychological trauma. I have had guests from home who would stare at the pile of dollars on the table, as if they were abandoning their firstborn.

It is well known that restaurant staff in the United States are poorly paid and live on tips. But the expectation of receiving something that is by definition left to the customer's discretion is irksome nevertheless and reveals the sentimental drama that takes place in American restaurants for what it is—a theatrical production. On occasion, I admit, I have been tempted to argue the point. But I have never worked up sufficient courage. I've always been afraid that Chuck (or Sharon, or Ed, or Brenda) would look at me with those big round eyes and tell me the story of his (or her) life again.

. . .

"NOSTALGIA STARTS IN the belly," Che Guevara used to say. The South American guerrilla leader's mind may have drifted off to the barbecued steaks of his native Argentina during the long nights on the Sierra Madre, and expatriate Italians can sympathize, even if their own longings take the more modest form of a cappuccino and a croissant, or perhaps just a good old-fashioned espresso.

The absence of any bars worthy of the name is one of the most painful aspects of life abroad for us. As an antidote to homesickness, Italians insist on drinking their coffee standing up in Vienna or Paris, inducing other customers to suspect that their watering-hole is frequented by the mentally disturbed, and annoying the owner, who thinks it is a trick to avoid paying the surcharge for table service. Another Italic obsession is the *espresso all'italiana*, which we demand in the certain knowledge that the beverage proffered will be an improbable blend of cough mixture and hemlock.

When this happens, we Italians abroad do not restrict ourselves to a grimace and a swift retreat. We dig our heels in and engage in lengthy learned debates on the relative merits of coffee in Turkey (too thick), France (too slow to prepare), and Great Britain. We attempt to convince the British that the liquid they call coffee is not such a bad drink but they really will have to find another name for it. Pride prevents us from admitting anyone else makes coffee like us. Our bars and our coffee-roasters have spoiled us.

In the United States, such conceit is out of place. Not only is it very easy to find a good espresso but Americans are doing with coffee what they have already done with pizza—they've fallen in love—and they're claiming to have invented it themselves. As far as coffee goes, it has to be admitted that they do have a certain track record. The first cafeteria was opened in Chicago around 1890, and the name was borrowed from Cuban Spanish (the owner insisted on the spelling *cafitiria*). Similar locales turned out to be so popular that even the name was imitated and extended to caketeria (for cakes), shaveteria (for barber's shops), drugetaria, and beauteria right through to the spine-chilling casketeria (a funeral parlor, from casket).

One hundred years on, coffee has outstripped all other hot drinks. The most popular version is still the weak coffee, or dirty water, against which generations of Italians have struggled in vain. In comparison with its British cousin, this coffee is technologically more advanced (no depressing teaspoons of instant, which have been replaced by a huge range of hardware), as well as more dangerous and much less seemly. While the British like drinking their lukewarm coffee in porcelain coffee cups, Americans take theirs at volcanic temperatures in those deadly polystyrene beakers or in mugs decorated with hobgoblins, cartoon characters, superheroes, or snappy one-liners. In America, government ministers see nothing embarrassing in sipping their coffee from a receptacle with I BOSS! YOU NOT! written on the outside. Captains of industry can flaunt a personal mug bearing the likenesses of the Three Little Piglets and still look their peers unswervingly in the eye.

The current recreational drug of choice, however, is espresso, and often excellent espresso, as we have noted. I have been approached in bars and asked in a conspiratorial whisper, "How many shots?" The enquiry refers to the number of coffees the customer intends to drink at once (an Italian-style coffee is one shot, a *caffè doppio* is two shots, and so on up to what is known in Italy as an *overdose*). One new, and deeply perturbing, fashion is to ask for a caffeinated coffee. This is a precaution against being served a decaf, for those citizens (and there are many) who need caffeine to keep going.

Coffee has also made its triumphal entrance into TV shows, the most reliable guide to the humors of the nation. Countless scenes in "Friends," "Frasier," and "Ellen" are shot in coffeehouses. In the series "Lois and Clark," Clark Kent's girlfriend orders a "short, nonfat mocha, decaf, no foam, no sugar, no whipped" (or in other words a strong, decaffeinated mocha-style coffee with no fat, foam, sugar, or whipped cream). At the celebrated Seattle-based Starbucks chain, they hand out leaflets illustrating all the possible combinations, and explaining the pronunciation: caf-ay´ la´-tay (*caffè latte*), caf-ay´ mo´-kah (*caffè moka*), caf-ay´ a-mer-i-cah´-no (*caffè americano*), and esspress´-o cone pa´-na (*espresso con panna*).

The biggest success of recent years has been the *cappuccino* (cap-uh-cheè-no), particularly after a meal, which indicates a certain confusion on the subject. The triumphant progress of cappuccino in the American language (it sneaked into the dictionary for the first time about 1950) and the impressive prices it commands—two or three times what you pay for an ordinary coffee—defy explanation. One reason could be the Chardonnay effect, a wine whose popularity among the English-speaking peoples is entirely due to its delightfully sensuous name. If that is indeed the case, then Americans don't order a cappuccino to drink it. They drink it for the fun of ordering it. Perverse? You betcha.

• • •

I AM OFTEN aware—in a shop, a lift, a restaurant, or a church—
of being the only person dressed like an American in Levi's, a
Gap shirt, and Timberland shoes. Nowadays the local fauna has
a vaguely European look. Generously cut trousers or tight skirts
all betray their origin, and their wearers' aspirations. Department
store–bought with European-sounding names that no one in Europe has ever heard of.

The same thing happens in restaurants. We new arrivals try to
find basic U.S. food ("Searchin' for a corner cafe/Where hamburgers sizzle on/an open grill night and day," Chuck Berry,
1959). But Americans crave new experiences and experiment
endlessly. It's no longer just a name game, testifying honestly to
past waves of immigration (French fries, English muffins,
Swedish meatballs, Polish sausage). Now exotic-tasting sauces
from Mexico, Indochina, or the Middle East garnish even the sacred burger. European beers with unpronounceable (for Americans, at any rate) names are threatening Budweiser and
Michelob, those deliciously taste-free beverages that are wildly
popular in Europe.

Nevertheless, there is one day of the year when the role
switching stops and that is the Fourth of July. On America's birthday, everything is clear. Americans behave like Americans. We—
partly out of politeness and partly out of envy—ape them.

• • •

I CONFESS THAT I had done my homework. I had read, asked
questions, and listened. I had found out that on the Fourth of July
America—even the America of Washington—remembers that it

is an extraordinarily dynamic, vibrantly alive, and superbly kitsch land. The Fourth of July—I was assured—is a fair held by a village with 250 million residents, where fireworks, barbecues, beer, and sweaty bodies are the order of the day. Fine, I said. This cynical European is going to have a day out.

However, you can't watch the Fourth of July. You have to take part. The day begins in the same way as New Year's Eve in Italy. With the odd premature explosion as a trial rocket is launched into the damp air by some impatient patriot. In homes, preparations are under way for the traditional picnic, which can last all day. Lots of families wait for dark to fall—and the fireworks display—while sitting on the grass. Fathers will be lost in an alcohol-induced stupor. Children will be playing frisbee or football. Mothers will be silently checking the contents of the picnic basket.

Thirty-fourth Street is in no hurry, and things get under way about six o'clock in the evening. Dave and the other students, full of enthusiasm and bad intentions, load their girlfriends and beer onto a Jeep. Other staunchly Democratic neighbors set off for private picnics where they can be sure they won't meet the masses they so passionately defend. With Anna and Massimo, two friends who have just arrived from Milan, we try to find a spot on the mall. No way. A huge crowd has been waiting for hours and there is a patchwork of brightly colored tablecloths marking off the territorial claims of their owners. Our friends from Milan suggest a restaurant. I reply that this is America, and persuade them to carry on.

We have to queue to reach the banks of the Potomac River and decide to look for a spot on the Virginia side. Here too, the chaos is quite superb. Cars are parked Italian-style on the grass of the central reservation and the riverside lawns are scarred by tire marks. Radios blast out unrecognizable pop songs and beefy young men throw footballs and tackle each other on the table-cloths. Baseballs whiz through the air to unknown destinations. Cyclists in one-piece phosphorescent sportswear speed along the asphalt while the aromas of barbecues and beer—the mainstays of the day's menu—fill the air. There is not one square inch of ground free. Our friends from Milan suggest we go home. I reply that this is America, and persuade them to carry on.

It cannot be said that we pass unobserved. We are wearing white linen and dragging with us a wicker basket that looks quin-tessentially English. At a Glyndebourne concert, it would be im-peccable but in the present context, it seems faintly provocative. After much searching, we find three free square meters under a tree near the river. The tree is the reason why this space was left free for it obscures part of the view of the sky over the mall, and Americans refuse to compromise when it comes to views. Since views are free, why settle for a partly obscured one? Anna and Massimo look around, observe our neighbors, and propose beat-ing a dignified retreat. It is no place for the faint-hearted, I admit. But this is America, I say, and persuade them to stay.

We lay out our tablecloth, make the sandwiches and drink blood-temperature Budweiser. The sun disappears behind us and the spotlights that illuminate Washington's monuments come on. After three beers, American neoclassical architecture is a mov-ing sight. Anna has opened a can of Spam. She tries it, and tells us, charitably, that it is ham mousse. The boats on the river take up position to watch the fireworks. The motor yachts of the rich and the smaller vessels of the less privileged find a common bond in the alcohol level of their passengers, joined in the vibrant, but debatable, democracy of drink.

At the appointed hour, the firework display starts. Miracu-lously, the ghetto-blasters fall silent—or else are drowned by the noise of the exploding rockets. The crowd watches in orderly, open-mouthed admiration. The Washington of muggers and street-fighting demonstrators lies back on the grass, making whispered comments on the show and handing 'round the last snacks. This is an America that warms your heart. It is the united, unpretentious, honest country that exists only in schoolbooks and presidential addresses. And it is here, this evening, on a dark riverbank. Our friends from Milan are no longer suggesting that we should leave—mainly because they are asleep, having succumbed to jet lag.

August

*I*f you arrive in Washington during August, there's only one thing to do. Leave, and come back in October. In August, the heat is oppressive, the air is unbreathable, and the humidity is unbearable. The parks are luxuriant with vegetation but empty of people and unwelcoming. The sun, instead of shining the way it does in a child's drawing, hides behind an oily mantle of cloud. Washington in August is like living under the greasy glass top of a pinball machine. It is no longer fun to be there.

So, what do Italian tourists do in August? They arrive in droves, of course. I'll admit that we were responsible for some of those arrivals. My wife adores houseguests, because she loves spoiling them. And I adore guests too, because I love observing them. It's a minor perversion of which I am not proud, but which I have been cultivating for some time. Guests, and their habits, challenge the certainties of the household, which is a good thing.

Italians, for example, love strolling through the center of town. And it is perfectly pointless to explain that in the United States there are two crucial things missing. A town center and a street to stroll down. At a certain time of day, downtowns all over the States empty, and become dangerous places to be. People—the kind of people you want to meet—go home to the suburbs. "But what's the fun in walking round the suburbs?" complain our guests. Never mind, I say. Nobody walks in America. If you want to go for a stroll, put a sweatband around your head and pretend you've been jogging.

Nevertheless, guests are rarely convinced. Like children in a Dickens novel, they stare out of the window as evening falls, absolutely convinced that everybody—except them—is strolling up and down the boulevards of Washington.

• • •

WE ITALIANS ARE good at adapting to new environments and new situations. Put one of my fellow citizens in a German railway carriage and three hours later he or she will have found out the family histories of all the other passengers (obviously, it doesn't matter if they don't know the language). After two days in a Russian hotel, an Italian will be on first-name terms with the porter. Trapped in a waiting room full of Americans, an Italian will emerge with four addresses, two dinner invitations, and a souvenir baseball cap.

The only aspect of the journey that defeats my fellow citizens has an English name in Italian—*jet lag*. This "exhaustion, discomfort etc. resulting from the body's inability to adjust to the rapid changes of time zone necessitated by high-speed long-distance air travel" (as one Italian dictionary puts it) is a common malady among my fellow citizens. In fact, we're going to have to find a name for it in Italian that you can finish saying before the plane lands in the States.

Jet lag, I confess, has always intrigued me. The ruminations that follow have no scientific basis. They are mere observations. First of all, it is my conviction that the degree of misery induced is directly proportional to the individual's awareness of the phenomenon. In other words, if you've never heard of jet lag, you won't suffer from it. But anyone who has read thirty articles and is constantly brooding on the subject is going to have problems. The individuals most at risk are those who use the various anti–jet-lag techniques, such as trying to sleep during the flight, staying awake, eating, not eating, relaxing, or doing some physical activity or other. (If you see someone pointing their toes, clenching their fists, or rotating their head, don't worry. It's an anti–jet-lag exercise, not rigor mortis.)

Both schools of thought are fascinating. I know seventy-year-olds who refuse to admit that there is such a thing as jet lag and, no matter where they go, appear to be immune. They sleep like babies on their first night in Hong Kong and dine happily after an eight-hour flight to New York. But I also know healthy forty-year-olds who hobble off the plane in a pitiful condition. In the last four months, my friends and acquaintances have described to me all the symptoms in the medical dictionary, and some that aren't. I've listened to husbands telling their wives about strange disorders that the poor women, evidently used to the hypochondria of the Italian male, had to pretend to take seriously ("No, dear. I don't think itching is one of the symptoms of jet lag") while explaining that "allow one day for each hour's difference in time zone" is just a rule of thumb. There's no reason to be staggering round the house as if you've been poleaxed a week after you landed.

After a number of studies, of an anthropological rather than physiological nature, I have come to the following conclusion— the time difference between Italy and the East Coast of the

United States (six hours) is trivial. When you fly west, all you have to do is stay awake a little longer. And on the return journey, you merely need to refrain from collapsing onto the bed while mumbling what time it is in New York over and over again.

I suspect that Italians actually adore the time difference, even as they suffer from its effects. Some enjoy complaining. Others appreciate the alibi when they phone home at inconvenient hours. ("Darling! Don't tell me I woke you up! What's that? It's four in the morning?") A few like to be able at last to show off those ridiculous watches that display two times simultaneously, and some think it's an interesting topic of conversation. I must have heard the phrase "What time will it be in Italy now?" dozens of times. It never fails to annoy me. You're in America, for goodness' sake! Who cares what time it is in Italy?

But we do care. We care because the change of time zone induces that sense of wonder that makes Italians the world's eternal infants. We may be descendants of Leonardo Da Vinci but we're still not convinced that while it's Saturday night in Washington, in Milan it really is Sunday morning.

• • •

ONE OF THE discoveries that I love to point out to friends (even though I've only been here for four months—we Italians like to show we know the ropes) is the fundamental concept of air miles. A literal interpretation of the term fails to do it justice. Air miles are a currency, a fashion, a drug, and—according to the advertising industry—very sexy. They constitute an offer no one can refuse.

So, what exactly are these air miles? Some readers will already

know. They are points you accumulate by traveling with a particular airline, after joining their frequent-flyer scheme, and they allow you to get free air tickets. Similar promotions have arrived in
Italy (Alitalia has *Millemiglia*), but they don't excite quite the
same tingle as the real thing. Americans lose all composure at the
prospect of air miles. The only people who are worse behaved are
foreign residents, who lose their dignity as well as their composure.

Before we describe these excesses, it will be useful to explain
how the schemes work. The basic mechanism is simple. The airlines offer a certain number of points (called miles) for each flight
to maintain customer loyalty. The points vary depending on the
distance traveled and the class of ticket. Let's take economy on
United Airlines, whose program is called Mileage Plus. If you fly
from Washington to Chicago, you get 612 miles. Chicago-Seattle
is worth 1,720, and Washington-Milan 4,237. When you have a
certain number of miles, you are entitled to a free flight—twenty
thousand for a domestic journey and forty thousand for a flight to
Europe.

Thus far, no problem. But the mechanism has been complicated with a whole raft of new rules. Air miles can be added by
flying with associated nondomestic airlines. The free tickets can't
be used on certain days. Then there are various levels of loyalty
that entitle you to certain privileges. When you pass twenty-five
thousand miles, United Airlines promotes you to Premier, which
means you can check in at the Connoisseur desk. Note the
French names. To American ears, they suggest luxury and ele-
gance.

Seeing air miles were such a success, others have got in on the
game. AT&T, for example, offers five air miles for each dollar of
your phone bill. American Express will give you a mile for every

dollar you put on their plastic. Car rentals, hotels, shipping companies, and flower delivery services all tempt you with miles you can use with your favorite airline. These incentives work. Several studies have shown that the word *miles* exercises an attraction that *discount* has lost.

Perhaps it's because the frequent-flyer schemes have the same fascination as collecting bubblegum cards and trigger the same childish instincts—hoarding, the desire to win a prize, and the satisfaction of getting something for nothing. We foreigners, I repeat, behave worse than the locals do. I know people (grown-ups, or at least that's what they look like) who deliberately add many hours on to their journeys in order to fly with the same airline (and so clock up miles), or always use the same car rental firm so they don't miss the five-hundred-mile bonus.

Inevitably, I have been sucked in. Ruthlessly, I enrolled my parents in the Mileage Plus scheme to get half of their miles when they came to see us in America. I was horrified to find myself greedily totting up the coupons that entitle you to free flights (they're called checks). Many other Europeans behave like me. Washington's nights are peopled by British journalists and German diplomats calling the airlines to find out if their last flight from Boston has been logged and if they now have enough miles to take the family on a trip to Disneyworld.

In practice, when we come up against these novelties we realize that the United States is not the only nation of closet teenagers. It's a universal phenomenon. If in Europe we are reluctant to behave in a certain way, it doesn't prove that we are more serious. It simply shows that we are incapable of inventing such exciting pastimes.

• • •

ONE WAY OF distracting the attention of houseguests from the twin obsessions of the torrid climate and air-conditioning is to take them on a trip out of town. Virginia and Maryland, the states that border on Washington, may not be California or Arizona but they do offer many points of interest (seventeen in Maryland and sixty-two in Virginia, according to the American Automobile Association, which has counted them). These range from George Washington's residence, to settlements from frontier days, the Blue Mountains, and Atlantic beaches.

Italians in general, and this Italian in particular, are happy to take what comes. This country is fascinating not only for its spectacular aspects but also for its everyday routine. To love America, it's not enough to appreciate the natural beauty or the architectural heritage. You also need a special predilection for the obvious and, sometimes, for the horrific. In other words, you very soon become unable to live without America's sheer predictability.

Motels, to take one example. I'm not the only European whose jaw drops in wonder every time they enter a motel room. And I never cease to be amazed by how absolutely, impeccably, stunningly identical they are. The two queen-size beds (too big for one, too narrow for two). The bizarre flesh color of the telephone between the beds. The nylon sheets. The fitted carpet. The old wood-colored television that harks back to the days when TVs tried to blend in with the furniture. The remote control tied to the set so the guests can't slip it into their suitcase. The air-conditioning, with its COLD-WARM and OFF-FAN-A/C settings. The chain on the door. And the ever-present ice machine sitting outside, like some large, ungainly abandoned pet.

The genuine plastic, marble-effect washbasin is usually outside the bathroom. The bathroom light switch is always on your right as you go in. It's at hand level. (Americans go mad in Europe when they have to run their hands over acres of wall in the dark as if they were looking for a secret passageway.) The toilet bowl will have the customary strip of paper promising perfect hygiene. (I know of one writer who likes to cut the strip with a pair of scissors while saying, "I now declare this WC officially open.") The showers are identical, too, from Virginia to Oregon. When I found one that had different knobs, I made a note of the place and date—Howard Johnson motel, Whyteville, Virginia. August 27.

Europeans in America quickly get used to this standardization. After all, the world is still a beautiful and varied place even if the light switch is always in the same place. If you're from Italy, where many people spend their entire lives trying to find one thing they can depend on, then you adapt even more readily. Soon, the word *motel* ceases to conjure up images of suburban decay or clandestine lovers' trysts and acquires the connotations that render it so attractive to the locals—reassurance.

When you realize for the first time that you are experiencing this sensation, that's when you know you've caught the American disease. The sight of a neon sign by the side of the road will give you a feeling of relief. The Best Western shield, the yellow sun of Day's Inn, or the blue and white emblem of a Howard Johnson will elicit a childlike contentment at the end of a long day on the road.

The pleasures of absolute predictability begin when you check in to a motel. You can do this at any time of the day or night, and there is no need for the elaborate rituals that make life in Europe so exhausting. All you need is a credit card, an address, and a license plate number (which Italians, for some mysterious reason, are quite incapable of remembering). No one will carry your cases, while you rummage through your pockets for a small enough banknote to hand over as a tip. No bright young man will attempt to earn the aforementioned gratuity by explaining how to turn on the television and open the curtains, insulting your intelligence in the process. You can be under the shower ten minutes after you walk up to the desk. Fifteen minutes, and you can be wrapped up in the usual five towels, stretched out on a bed, watching the familiar TV set with an equally familiar can of Coca-Cola on a no less familiar bedside table. Your car is parked outside the room door, where it will spend the night, tethered like a cowboy's horse.

• • •

FOREIGNERS IN AMERICA learn to recognize other things apart from motel signs. The same hypnotic effect is exercised on the traveler by gas stations and fast food outlets. They are the oases and pyramids of the American landscape—places of refreshment and proof of permanence.

The outskirts of the cities change continuously but the Texaco stations and McDonald's restaurants are always the same. In Italy, McDonald's might be seen as a dangerously threatening innovation but in America, these places of refreshment are reassuringly traditional. It is no coincidence that McDonald's makes a point of telling you how many customers it has ("Over five billion served") nor that one of its slogans is "What you want is what you get." It's a way of saying there won't be any surprises, traps, rip-offs, or suspicious European food.

For those on the freeways at night, the well-known neon signs—America's most effective transquillizer—are the signal. New arrivals gradually learn the message. The big yellow M (McDonald's). The name of a beer in a distant window (Coors, Budweiser, Miller Lite). A red-and-white shack (Pizza Hut). These are not polite invitations. They are orders.

One travel writer, Bill Bryson, admits to being unable to resist the signs that say MCDONALD'S EXIT HERE on freeways. "Over and over through the weeks I found myself sitting at plastic tables with little boxes of food in front of me which I don't want or have time to eat, all because a sign had instructed me to be there." The food itself is another attraction. McDonald's hamburgers don't taste of hamburger. They taste of hamburger-from-McDonald's, which is an entirely different thing. Luigi Barzini, in his book, *O America!*, had this to say about another American food, "Everyone, at first, manages to distinguish the chemical taste from the real taste but, with the passage of time, fiction becomes reality."

Gas stations also attract foreigners. It's not merely a question of the influence of the cinema (the gas station, like the bedroom, is a classic scene in American films). Nor is it because the gas station is one of the places where America meets and falls into a democratic line. Young and old, rich and poor, ancient Dodge trucks and shiny new Lexuses all drink at the same (oil) well. You go up to the pump, select the right kind of gas (83, 87, 89 octane), pull the handle, wait for the counter to go back to zero, fill your tank, raise the handle, and go inside to pay amid mountains of candy bars, chewing gum, sodas, and cookies. Throughout this operation, tenured professors from Turin, ruthless Roman businesswomen, and—of course—callow journalists from Lombardy have a fine time. It's like being young again, when the prospect of being a gas station attendant, a car mechanic, or a firefighter held a justifiable fascination.

• • •

MANY ITALIANS THINK that a real American holiday means renting a mobile home and doing impressions of a trucker—ten thousand kilometers (over six thousand miles) in a month, short stops, and a splendid collection of states visited. Mobile homes, which Americans also call RVs, or recreational vehicles, look as if they are the ideal way to see a country the size of a continent and keep to a minimum any contact with hotel porters/waiters/ reception clerks, most of whom have the disadvantage of only speaking English and being only marginally interested in making the acquaintance of a family from Bologna.

I know precisely what I am talking about because I am one of those who have helped to make America's rental agencies the solid businesses they are today. I have traveled by mobile home with five friends (1977), one brother (1980), two parents (1987), and a wife (1992). I have also helped a sister, brother-in-law, and two nephews to organize a similar holiday. Each time, I have met a few Italians and lots of Americans who were traveling the same way.

Let me say straight away that I feel more in tune with people from my own country. It seems to me that Italians in an RV are people who are basically normal, generally calm, and happy with their lot—a country that has no narrow lanes or bottlenecks, gentle bends, and generously proportioned car parks. After a few days, Italian-filled vehicles take on a vaguely gypsy-esque aspect that is not unpleasant. You can sometimes see them parked at night in badly lit lay-bys along the freeways. The guardian angel of Italians abroad—a resourceful lad if ever there was one—is watching over them. If a German family were to be equally foolhardy, they would be mugged, if not worse.

Americans with motor homes, the legendary RV people, are a very different kettle of fish. First of all, they are brilliantly organized. The American Automobile Association supplies them with detailed maps and guides that tell them if a particular motel in Gold Beach, Oregon, will take pets, or whether a restaurant in

South Carolina gives discounts to AAA members. If they indicate their precise itinerary, they can get a ring binder (called a Trip-Tik) that contains a personalized route. At any given moment, the driver will know exactly how far away he or she is from the nearest gas station or parking area. As all these documents are free, American tourists are laden like pack mules when they leave home and spend whole days leafing through pages that describe sights they will never see, since they are too busy to actually look out of the window.

These masters of the road marathon often travel in gigantic vehicles that are out of all proportion to their real needs. Forget those tiny campers that Germans bring to the Italian Riviera or Lake Garda. A family-size motorhome is a thirty-foot-long, self-propelled house. The more luxurious models are oceanliners on wheels. Every time I see one pull up, I expect a three-ring circus, complete with horses, to get out. After a long wait—RV people are never in a hurry—I find myself staring at two frail pensioners who could probably sleep in the glove compartment.

The more perverse RVers hitch their car to their motorhome and drag it round the United States like a dinghy. These are the same individuals who fill their vehicle with useless contraptions that go way beyond the mere microwaves or TV sets that are now fitted as standard in all models. The real professionals have videos, ice machines, and electric can openers to turn their RV into a motorhome-from-home. It is a perfect example of the dreams of a nation that wants it all. Just as many Americans expect to be able to eat what they feel like yet not put on weight, others want to go where they want while staying at home. Unfortunately, they often manage to do so. So we find ourselves stuck behind them on the freeways as they dutifully observe the 55-mph speed limit. And what's worse, when we overtake them they wave at us.

• • •

I DON'T KNOW if you've ever been in a pancake house, one of those places where Americans devour breakfasts that would feed a busload of Italians. They are not outstandingly elegant places. At eight in the morning you can cut the smell of frying fat with a knife, people smoke, and the waitresses shout "Honey" then invite you to get the heck out of the way.

It's now Sunday morning. We got here yesterday from Washington to spend the weekend and this pancake house, a term we might translate into Italian as *casa della crêpe* if we were somewhere a little more sophisticated than Ocean City, Maryland. The place is crowded. The customers are mainly families. The men have disturbing tattoos, the women have the bewildered eyes of girls who have grown up too fast, and their blond-haired children are happily eating fries and eggs drowned in butter adrift on oceans of grease. The America of diets and calorie counters is light-years away. People come here to fill their bellies, not to have something to talk about.

It is fascinating, and eerily moving, to observe these family meals. The early settlers could not have imagined that their new homeland would one day sire progeny like this. Yet here is this white underclass, with its dilapidated motorcars and families even less roadworthy than their automobiles. These are poor people—the uninsured America that Bill Clinton hoped to help through health reform—but they are also strangely, absolutely, magnificently American.

Shortly, these families will get into their cars outside the pancake house and drive along the coast of Maryland and Delaware, without exceeding the speed limit. They'll pull up and pay to leave their car at one of the parking lots, then spend their time doing one of those melancholy activities that Americans have classified as entertainment, after having first given them an attractive name. Beach-combing, or looking for objects on the beach. Clamming, which means digging in the sand for shellfish. Or perhaps stormwatching, which is just looking at the sea when it's too rough to bathe in. When it's time to eat, they'll get out their bags of food. They'll eat (badly), without leaving any litter. They'll drink (too much), without leaving any empty beer cans behind. Then they'll go back to Philadelphia and Baltimore, the young wife driving with the infinitely sad face of a minor saint.

Of course, they are in no sense exemplary. H. L. Mencken—a brilliant, all-American Voltaire who was born right here in Maryland—wrote that "on certain levels of the American race, indeed, there seems to be a positive libido for the ugly." Fifty years later, this underclass has proved him right. Nevertheless, these are people who behave with decency. It may well be that there is no choice for there is also a United States in uniform that takes speed limits and parking restrictions extremely seriously. But we Italians are still impressed. The mere fact of being American— even when America has given you very little—seems to imply a sort of mystic consensus. The fact that you are Italian—even when Italy has given you everything—for many of my compatriots doesn't appear to mean anything at all.

September

*W*hen foreigners think of America, they all have the same place in mind. It's not Manhattan. It's not Hollywood. It's not even the Grand Canyon. The place we are thinking about is a quiet road where the neighbors say "Hi" to each other, dogs sniff but don't bark, and in the evening, all the lights come on at the same time. Do you remember the house that comes on screen between scenes in TV serials? It sparkles in the daytime, is suffused in a soft blue light in the evening, it's surrounded by greenery in the summer and snow-covered in winter. When I was younger, I used to think it was always the same house. Only the TV series changed.

It has to be said that Washington is not the ideal place to make these childhood fantasies come true. The capital of the United States is not going through one of its better periods. The middle classes have fled to the suburbs and the city's resident population has fallen from 1965's 800,000 to the present 580,000. The town is close to bankruptcy. One person in four lives below the federal poverty level. A convicted drug offender is about to become mayor. And then there is the not insignificant detail that Washington vies with Chicago as the nation's most violent conurbation. Today, it has the third-highest number of murders of all America's cities.

But dreams—especially foreigners' dreams—die hard. The northwestern part of Washington is relatively peaceful, and Georgetown has stayed the way it was when Guido Piovene forty years ago called it, "the most refined neighborhood of the city, where a pastel pink sky shines over rows of small houses." On the third Thursday of each month, the *Washington Post* publishes a list of the crimes committed in the city (location, crime, and victim) but Georgetown fills only one column. One or two break-ins and the odd mugging but no shootings in the street, as happens elsewhere in Washington.

The houses (three thousand of them—they're very precise about such things here) have that special grace all old things in America are endowed with. "They are white for the most part, some are painted red, or yellow, or green, and almost all are in the noble Georgian style," Piovene adds. They look like "a childhood dream, that brings to mind the paintings of the American primitive artists." The streets, like those in Great Britain, betray a certain lack of maintenance. Here and there can still be seen gas lamps and the tramlines that fill our hearts with nostalgia and slash our car tires. Years ago, Georgetown residents voted against a subway. They prefer the district to remain historic and charming, as the local tourist guides and newspapers (*The Georgetowner* and *The Georgetown Current*) like to put it.

We now feel quite at home in this corner of America (zipcode 20007). Once a month, the residents' association invites us to a meeting by introducing a postcard decorated with balloons and flowers under our front door. For some time, the shopkeepers have given the impression of recognizing us. At Neam's, the tiny supermarket with the big, big prices, the owner smiles, especially when I take his advice on wine purchases. When we go to the New York Cleaners (ninety-nine cents for a shirt, which my wife claims is one of Western civilization's major achievements), the seriously corpulent African American proprietor says, "Good to see you" without taking her eyes off the television and then asks me if I'm Greek.

In Georgetown, new arrivals can forget about the comfortable anonymity of the big cities. If you want a break from the pressure of Italian courtesy, this is the wrong place to be. Our neighbors are polite and generous with helpful advice but also prove to possess the terrifyingly good memory for first names shared by most of their compatriots. A typical conversation when we bump into one might go like this:

"Beppe, Ortensia! Great to see you! How're you doing?"

I realize that I can't remember the name of the woman, whom I must have met briefly months ago. I shoot a worried glance at my wife, who is always ready to abandon me to my fate in these circumstances.

"Not bad, thanks. And you?" I answer, blessing the English language and its generic second-person pronoun.

"Fantastic. Couldn't be better. Did you know Paul changed his job?"

To know whether Paul has changed job, it might be useful to know who Paul is, and what job he used to do. However, you can't ask these details. My tactic, at moments like this, is to say something in reply and repeat the name "Paul" furiously, so that I'll remember it in future.

"Paul? Really? Paul? Paul changed his job? Good for Paul. See you soon. All the best to Paul."

Obviously, you can't always get out of trouble quite so easily. I have spent whole evenings at a dinner trying to remember the name of the woman sitting next to me, who has been telling me about her first marriage. This intimacy naturally excludes the possibility of retreating onto the neutral ground of "ma'am." The little verbal tricks I learned in England, I have to concede, do not work in the United States. American sincerity is a steamroller. These people are professionals of etiquette who play strictly hardball. My masterstroke—always greeting people with "Nice to see you" and never with "Nice to meet you," which implies that I am seeing them for the first time—is a run-of-the-mill trick that even itinerant vacuum-cleaner sellers have dropped.

My neighbors, I fear, have cottoned on to these clumsy ruses. But they don't seem to mind, and assume they are an entertaining European idiosyncrasy. They continue to be extremely friendly, and continue to put me on the spot. For instance, the woman who lives opposite has lovely twins—a boy and a girl whose names I will never be able to remember. The students from New England who live next door asked our permission before putting up an American flag in front of the house, which they lower every evening like a well-drilled army barracks. Our other neighbor, the allergy specialist, made a few aristocratic protests before surrendering to the magnolia in our garden that discharges tons of leaves into his swimming pool. For some time now, he has been listening to South American music at all hours. I suppose there are worse ways he could try to get his own back.

. . .

RELATIONSHIPS ARE GOOD with the rest of the neighbors and conversation comes easily. Americans tell you more about themselves in an hour than the British do in ten years. The main thing is not to mistake this cordiality for friendship. It's more a sort of cosmetic to perk up everyday life, and should be treated as such.

There are three main topics of conversation in and around number 1513. Garbage, wild animals, and gardening.

Garbage is, without a doubt, the Problem with a capital P. Because of its chronic lack of funds, the local administration tends to leave our rubbish where it is. Any excuse will do—a public holiday, a strike, a downpour, or a traffic jam. In other parts of Washington, the presence of heaps of colored plastic sacks would pass unobserved and in some areas of New York, they would even blend in with the surroundings. But in Georgetown, this corner of Old America, the garbage bags are obvious after one day, unpleasant after two days, offensive after three, and downright disgusting after a week.

The arbiters of our fate are the operatives of the sanitation department. Generally, these are muscular young black men who arrive clinging onto a decrepit garage truck that pumps out earsplitting rap music. Most sport handkerchiefs tied pirate-style around their heads. They jump down from the still-moving truck, exchange a few guttural syllables, and examine our heap of bags with a skeptical air. Anxious eyes watch from every window. Everyone is hoping to be the lucky one today. In the end, the pirate crew throws a few bags onto the garbage truck and leaves the rest. After they have gone, the street is covered with plastic bottles and cans, and looks as if a bomb has hit it.

As soon as the Tyrants of Trash have departed, professors, lawyers, journalists, and members of Congress emerge from the houses of Thirty-fourth Street to debate the following topic. What was their criterion for selection? How can we satisfy the aesthetic demands of the pirates? After six months, some conclusions appear inevitable.

a) The pirates have a thorough knowledge of the city garbage regulations. Anyone who puts glass in a black bag (it should go in the blue ones, along with plastic and aluminium), or paper in the white bags (its proper place is in the green boxes), is immediately disqualified.

b) The pirates are cunning. They know that the heavier black bags will contain grass, leaves, and earth, for whose removal the special pickup service should be called.

c) The pirates are well aware of their own bargaining power. They know that Thirty-fourth Street is populated by cowards, and that no one is ever going to come out to complain.

d) The pirates don't want to work.

The morning all the garbage lining Thirty-fourth Street was taken away without a murmur of complaint, the residents, moved almost to tears, were reminded of the title of an old film, *Miracle on 34th Street*. I won't forget that day in a hurry. It was mid-September, the leaves were turning russet, and there were no black bags under the blue American sky.

• • •

THE SECOND TOPIC of conversation is provided by the animals that are attracted by the garbage, especially when it's had time to ripen. We're not talking pets here. I don't mean the dogs that do no more than destroy flowerbeds and besmirch the footpaths. These are wild animals—real Discovery Channel stuff. Everyone except, apparently, your correspondent knows about their presence in the neighborhood.

A few days ago, I saw a belligerent-looking van bearing the legend *Opossum & Racoon Specialists* draw up outside our window. Curious about these ghostbusters of the animal kingdom, I asked them what brought them to Georgetown. The man at the wheel explained somewhat self-importantly, "Georgetown has the highest concentration of racoons in the United States of America." "I thought they lived in national parks," I said. The expert chose to ignore my comment. "And the possums? Have you seen any? They look like overweight rats, but they're not." Possums? I haven't seen any. I've seen some gray squirrels, a black squirrel, various species of birds, crickets, endlessly eloquent cicadas, and the occasional cat.

Nevertheless, the ghostbuster was right. A few evenings later, an obese murine—subsequently identified, thanks to the Encyclopedia Britannica, as a common opossum (*Didelphys marsupialis*)—trotted into the light under the streetlamps, crossed the road and wriggled under the gate into our garden. It was to return often on subsequent evenings, causing us a certain amount of apprehension. We didn't want it to end its days under the wheels of a car. The pirates from the sanitation department would have objected.

• • •

IMPATIENS IS NOT just the English name for the *fiori di vetro* flowers that I planted in front of the house last May. It's also a good description of how I feel. I have in the past often purchased flowers. On occasion, even grown them. Never have I planted them. That's one reason for my novice's enthusiasm. The other is fear of letting myself down in comparison with the Thirty-fourth Street professionals. Will they bloom? Will they wilt? Have I given them enough water? Have I drowned them, as my wife insists I have?

Without realizing, I have begun to read the gardening tips in the newspapers, something Americans regard as a sure sign of middle age (a typical gardener is between thirty-four and forty-nine years of age, has an income in excess of fifty thousand dollars per annum, and spends four hundred dollars a year on his or her hobby). Slowly, I develop a fierce hatred for the motorists who park too near to the curb, and for dogs that use my garden as a public convenience. The wife of the senator from Montana doesn't have these problems. She has screwed a brass plate to the foot of a tree. It says, "Please do not litter," and the dogs obey. They appear to recognize the senator's flowers.

This sudden passion for botany on the part of someone who until yesterday could not tell a sweet pea from a sunflower is not just an innocent eccentricity.

Looking after the little flowerbeds under the trees (tree-boxes) is a civic obligation in Georgetown. Evening after evening throughout the summer, I have tended the one in front of our house. I have dragged the garden hose out onto the street. I have administered evil-looking fertilizers. I have visited Johnson's— the amateur gardener's Mecca—and returned laden with pointless garden tools.

Over the last few days, I have received congratulations from several people. Not for the results, which continue to be modest and unlikely to open the portals of the Georgetown Garden Club, but for my progress. The tree-box in front of 1513 used to look like a garbage tip but now there are a dozen or so flowers peeking out. Americans appreciate these things. In Britain, the most popular gardening magazine is called *Home & Garden*. The American equivalent is *Better Homes & Gardens*, with the accent on improvement. I'm beginning to think I like this country.

The compliments were followed by greetings cards, phone calls, and one or two dinner invitations. When I asked the students to water the tree-box while I was away, they readily agreed.

Six months after moving to Thirty-fourth Street, I feel that I have been accepted. Of course, such acceptance is not automatic for Italians abroad. It doesn't matter how rich, sophisticated, or elegant we are. In the English-speaking world, our sense of civic responsibility is constantly under scrutiny. Years ago in London, my (American) landlord asked me not to hang my washing out from the window on a line, "the way you do in Italy." How did he know? He'd seen it in films, of course.

. . .

PLANT LIFE IN Thirty-fourth Street isn't limited to tree-boxes and small, hidden gardens. There is a green area between Q Street and Volta Place that goes under the name of Volta Park. To be honest, "park" is a bit of an overstatement. The area includes a small swimming pool, two tennis courts, two basketball courts, a playground, and some grass. Each of these sections has its own, well-defined, clientele. The swimming pool and the basketball courts are frequented mainly by black families and teenagers from other parts of Washington. Tennis players are mostly white for it is used by those local residents who are too poor or lazy to go all the way out to a country club. And thanks to the nearby Montessori nursery school, the playground looks like a miniature version of the United Nations General Assembly.

One day, a note pushed under our door announced that on the following Saturday the Volta Park Clean-Up would take place. This annual event is necessary because the perennially penniless District of Columbia administration makes no provision for maintenance. It was, the organizers informed us, a tradition and volunteers would be welcome. As new arrivals, we decided to take part. We turned up on time, dressed like Amish farmers in old trousers and faded jerseys, carrying hoes, spades, brushes, and pans.

I could see at once from the expressions of the others present that our zeal was appreciated. Everyone wanted to know where we lived, where we came from, what we did for a living, and, above all, what we were intending to do that afternoon: flowers, grass, or footpaths? We noted that there weren't very many volunteers— seven, in all—but we were assured that others were on the way. Nevertheless, it looked as though most of the residents had opted for a donation of cash or bulbs and then gone away for the weekend.

Most of the available labor was comprised of women of an undefinable age somewhere between forty-five and seventy-five. The blond hair and elegantly casual outfits have nothing in common with attributes of their Californian cousins, who would have transformed the occasion into an open-air exhibition of the plastic surgeon's art. Washington women have a different style but they do share one characteristic with California. They gossip. While I was trying to tear up the weeds tenaciously infesting the footpaths, I found out enough about my neighbors to fill three episodes of "Friends." World Bank employees waiting for their divorce. Diplomats' wives who had undergone artificial insemination. Doctors with difficult children. And a new arrival who had started a collection to fill Volta Park with Japanese cherry trees. He wasn't even from Japan.

Two hours later, we were on intimate terms. Not only did I know what had happened to the man at the World Bank (his wife left him), but I had also been introduced to a number of passersby ("This is our nice Italian worker"), some of whom looked exhausted from jogging but showed no inclination to bend over and pick up a hoe. One of the joggers tried to be polite and asked me if I was paid by the hour or the day. I said I was a slave and belonged to the woman at number 1506.

Every so often, my fellow workers—and sound track—would make an excuse, saying they had to go home, and come back a few minutes later. I didn't pay any attention at first but then I began to get suspicious. The only explanation was this. Their houses were close to where we were working. My workmates were therefore cleaning up in front of their own homes. And so I, by working in the same area, was cleaning their sidewalk.

The realization made a profound impression on me. Here, I wanted to shout, was a splendid lesson in American socialism! Here was proof that the country's two great passions—the desire for private ownership that drove the pioneers, and the spirit of cooperation that so impressed Alexis de Tocqueville—are not incompatible. All you need is a well-meaning Italian who is willing to work for nothing. I only hope that in commemoration of the afternoon's work and altruism, someone has put a plaque in a corner of Volta Park with the inscription:

HERE, WITH PICK AND HOE AND SHOVEL
DID ONE NAÏVE ITALIAN GROVEL
KNEELING OVER WEEDS TENACIOUS
HE LABORED, YET HIS SOUL WAS GRACIOUS.
OH STRANGER, TELL IT TO THE PRESS
THAT SEVERGNINI CLEANED THIS MESS.

• • •

ON SUNDAY MORNINGS, we go to Mass at Dahlgren Chapel on the Georgetown University campus. Until eleven o'clock, we read the gigantic Sunday papers, a pagan rite observed all over the English-speaking world. About midday, we leave the house, like the chemist and his wife in a short story by the Sicilian writer Giovanni Verga. It's a habit that troubles me not one whit. I have always believed that it is necessary to adapt to the rhythms of a country if you want to understand it. And Sunday morning, in the United States, exists for being tranquil. It's silly to get worked up. Trying to get something done at all costs is for tourists.

The stretch of road that separates us from the university is short. In this area, Georgetown looks almost shabby. The houses are smaller, their fronts brighter and grubbier. The flowerbeds contain empty beer cans as well as flowers.

This is student country, an ideal place to feel old at forty. But it's attractive, nonetheless. Eighteen-year-olds, with heavy-duty bags under their eyes, cast-off clothes, and seriously uncombed hair, ghost past, their gaze fixed firmly on the far horizon as they ponder the universe. Young women with no makeup flash past on bicycles to destinations we can only guess at. The cafeterias are full of people engaged in the very American pastime of consuming their Sunday breakfast, or in other words, eating too much on Sunday morning after drinking too much on Saturday night.

But our destination is Dahlgren Chapel on the university campus. Before June, we used to go to another church on Pennsylvania Avenue but we had to admit defeat. The priest's Irish accent, together with the worst acoustics in the history of Catholic architecture, proved too much. We discovered that the church had been attended by John and Jacqueline Kennedy, who had no problem with the Irish accent and lived not far away (first in a redbrick house at 3307 N Street and then in a white one at 1600 Pennsylvania Avenue).

Dahlgren Chapel is run by Jesuits, who also founded Georgetown University. It's a modern church and, apart from the occasional professor, nothing looks more than seventy years old. But it's friendly and, like all American churches of whatever denomination, demanding. It would be an exaggeration to say that the Roman Catholic religion has had to turn into a kind of Protestantism to survive, as Mario Soldati wrote in *America Primo Amore*. It is, however, true that Mass in America is not for spectators, as it is in some Italian churches where actually singing or saying the responses is considered a lack of respect.

In America, you either take part or you stay at home. Visiting Italian Catholics—even practicing ones—are shocked and amazed when they see the minor tour de force that is an American religious ritual. It has to be said that there is nothing gratuitously odd about it. You just can't afford to let your attention wander.

At the beginning of the service, the priest explains that an assembly of the faithful is not a group of strangers. He therefore invites everyone to introduce themselves. This operation, which in Italy would involve a brief *buongiorno* and in Germany a bare nod of the head (followed by a list of academic titles), is transformed in America into a sort of friendship-fest. Sunday after Sunday, I have met students from New Jersey, their parents, ex-alumni, nearly qualified doctors, and aspiring lawyers. To each, I have explained who I was and what I was doing in Washington, eliciting polite expressions of interest (one of the expatriate European's little luxuries—even the most ordinary activities acquire importance simply by crossing the Atlantic). The intimacy continues when the moment comes to exchange a sign of peace. Last week, a woman in front of me turned around and pounced on my neighbor, asking how his holiday had gone.

The community atmosphere is not limited to introductions (these can be a problem—once you've made someone's acquaintance, you want to continue the conversation during the service).

The Our Father is recited holding hands with the people next to you. There's also another prayer that is recited with one arm raised in a sort of Roman salute, the one that was popular under Fascism. (Oh, how fortunate America is not to share those memories!) And the musicians get a round of applause. I also remember the holiday tour-style promotion of spiritual retreats (five days, all-included.) and a snappy four-lesson method for learning how to read the Gospels.

On occasion, the priest will ask questions during the sermon, forcing the congregation to pay attention. During prayers, everyone has the opportunity to propose a topic. When this happens in Italy, the proposals made are usually honest but vaguely rhetorical (such as hopes for world peace, or an end to famine in Africa). But Americans invite you to pray for their friends and relatives, supplying name, surname, and appropriate personal details.

It is during communion that the difference between an American church and an Italian one really emerges. In the States, everything is beautifully choreographed. The communicants in the front pews get up, form a line in the center aisle, and go back to their places by filtering down the side aisles. When one row sits down, the next makes its move. Have you ever seen what happens in Italy? Everyone stands up at the same time, forming a dozen separate lines that engulf the pews like milk boiling over from a pan. Those returning to their seats—apparently absorbed in silent contemplation—bump into those who are still waiting in a spectacular indoor reenactment of the traffic jams that enliven the working week.

However, at the end of the service, Europeans cease to feel a mixture of embarrassment and awe, opting unreservedly for the latter. You see, in Italy, the announcement that the Mass is over produces an effect similar to that of a gunshot in a cattery. The faithful race outside, turning their backs abruptly on the celebrant as if he were a busboy in a greasy spoon diner. By the time the long-suffering priest has finally managed to utter the words "Go in peace," everyone is already outside or piling into the nearest café. In America, and not just at Dahlgren Chapel, the congregation sings the final hymn with gusto and waits respectfully until the priest has made his way to the door, where he will say his individual good-byes to everybody. Only at that point will the worshippers unhurriedly head for the door, and the rest of their Sunday.

October

A few days ago outside a supermarket called Rodman's (a sort of creatively chaotic drugstore where you can find anything, provided you aren't looking for it), an elderly woman asked me, "Could you please push back my car?" I promptly marched over to her Chrysler and took up the universally recognized position of push-starters everywhere. The woman looked at me pityingly. "I said 'cart,' not 'car,'" she murmured. It was at that point I realized that she had actually said *cart* because anglicized Italians, as well as the British, of course, indicate the object in question with the word *trolley*.

The example is banal. There have been hundreds of others, some with tragic consequences. One Japanese student was killed when he wandered into the wrong house and did not understand the order, "Freeze!" What is undeniable is that anyone who has learned English from the British will have to go through a delicate process of psychological adjustment on arriving in the United States.

To start with, it's not true that we don't understand Americans. If anything, they don't understand us. (Old English in the United

States is the name of a furniture wax.) It is well-known that if you pronounce the words *hot* and *water* the British way—that is, with short vowel sounds—you'll get uncomprehending looks in American restaurants. As long ago as 1942, the *Guide to Great Britain* prepared by the Ministry of War opened with the words, "At first you may not understand what they are talking about." But it's really no worse than that. When George Bernard Shaw, paraphrasing Oscar Wilde, said that Great Britain and the United States were two great nations divided by a common language, he demonstrated that he was an excellent coiner of aphorisms and an even better liar.

For those who, like the present writer, have learned their English in Great Britain, there are other difficulties. First, there is the dilemma of tuning your ear to some of the accents of the southern states (Virginia and all points south). There are actually two problems here. As well as the accent, there is the usage of black Americans, who often pronounce *ask* as if it was *ax* and substitute some finite forms of the verb to be (am, is) with *be* or adopt expressions that are grammatically questionable, not to mention physically alarming, such as "to hit someone upside the head." These challenges make my visits to the Exxon gas station on Wisconsin Avenue moments of intense emotion, with vaguely comic overtones. The African American attendant speaks and I continue to say, "Excuse me?" even when I do understand for the sheer pleasure of listening again to his stunningly unorthodox syntax.

Then again, one is almost ashamed to abandon the linguistic habits acquired in Great Britain. Using the word *trash* instead of *rubbish* to talk about the things you throw out feels like giving in. The temptation to say *lorry* and not *truck* is strong (although it helps to remember that *truck* comes from the Latin *trochus*). When America is a "second love," as the writer Mario Soldati put it, the lifts take a while to turn into elevators and a journey in someone else's car remains a lift and not a ride.

Until, that is, the day you feel silly asking for your customary bill in the restaurant. In Washington, Bill could be the cook's name but what you want is the check. So, it was wrong of me at the gas station to ask how much I had to pay for the petrol. The youth on duty at the pump stared at me as if I had just arrived on a bicycle and said, "Egad, sirrah, 'tis a sore task to propel this velocipede!" That was when I was converted. As usual, America had won.

• • •

THE BIGGEST PROBLEM of all for those arriving from Europe is understatement, a concept that quite simply does not exist in the United States. Americans, with one or two exceptions here and there in New York, Washington, or San Francisco, are unaware of the existence of such attenuated declarations. Overmodest affirmation engenders in them a feeling of vertigo. Even the metaphors are more robust in the States. The British storm in a teacup (the equivalent of an Italian storm in a glass of water) is transformed in America into a tempest in a teapot.

In the States, if you say you're not very good, it means that you are lacking in skill. Self-denigration, adored in London as the most sophisticated form of snobbery, is taken here as an admission of weakness. Or worse, as a sort of incomprehensible existential angst.

Over the last six months, I have made quite a few false impressions. When a dinner guest saw a book with my name on the cover on a bookshelf, he asked me, "Are you a good writer?" My British training got the better of professional vanity and I replied,

"Not really. I just give it a try." A fatal error. My guest was visibly disappointed and went off convinced he was wasting time with an amateur when he might have been able to tell his friends he had met a real European writer.

After that, I set myself a number of rules. Rule one: Be immodest. One excellent American writer, Russell Baker, claims to have learned the following proverb from his mother, "Blow your own horn because no one is going to blow it for you." "This is the American way," Baker continues. Boasting about your own good qualities is not easy, even for someone like your correspondent who has always shown a certain predisposition for the practice. But one has to learn. In a world happily divided into winners and losers, it's better, all things considered, to belong to the former category.

It takes time, but with a little effort, anyone can be a self-aggrandizer. After a while, one even begins to enjoy this psychological striptease where anything goes, including name-dropping, mentioning prizes and degrees, or describing one's comfortable financial position (this is a European's revenge on the country that refused to give him a credit card).

Reticence, part English-inspired and part church-induced, is soon cast aside. I have known Italians who, after a few years in the States, talk like Muhammad Ali ("I am the greatest!") and will have to spend time in a psychological decompression chamber before going back to Italy. Here, however, they do very well and have taught me lots of little tricks. It's crucial, for example, always to be serious. Saying how great you are and then bursting into laughter—which in London would be taken as a sign of a healthy attitude to life—will only convince people in Washington that you are an eccentric who might at any minute start writing on the mirrors or swallowing ashtrays.

Rule two: Remember that this is a rather coy nation, and that words can upset. An imperfect knowledge of English, coupled with Italian lack of sensitivity, can have disastrous results. Here are a few examples. In America, no one sweats. At worst, people perspire. Bodily functions are camouflaged behind a range of euphemisms. Even children and dogs go to the bathroom, despite the fact that the former wear diapers and the latter use our treebox. The bathroom itself, as Paul Watzlawick noted in *Gebrauchsanweisung für Amerika* (*America—Instructions for Use*), is always called the restroom, even though nobody goes there for a quiet lie-down.

Rule three: Avoid making clever remarks. Seventy-five percent of jokes are based on understatement. That concept is alien to American culture, so many of your jokes will not be understood. Which ones? The best ones, usually.

• • •

ANOTHER EQUALLY SERIOUS problem for new arrivals is learning how to defuse other people's politeness. Italians are generally enchanted at first by a country where everyone is smiling. Where everyone says thank you. Where after an hour a stranger is treating you as if you played together as children. Believing the range of polite forms in British English—a considerable arsenal, if the truth be told—to be insufficient, Americans have created their own progressive politeness scale. What happens is that the more a polite expression is used, the less effective and attractive it becomes, like overmasticated chewing gum. At that point, you have to find a new, prettier, and more telling turn of phrase. But that, too, will pall. And you'll need something stronger.

It's the same kind of addiction that ties people to alcohol or drugs. Here, though, the starting point is not a glass of whisky or a pill but a thank-you. Greetings and salutations, especially, have suffered this escalation. Americans don't even notice so it's we Europeans who find ourselves helpless and up to our necks in treacly sentiment. Let's take a sales assistant in a department store. She may be rude, if she's had an argument with her boyfriend. Or, as you take your leave, she may give you a dazzling smile accompanied by one or more of the following expressions: "Have a nice day," "Now you take care," or—an insidious new-comer—"Missing you already." It is easy to sympathize with young Italian males who get the wrong idea when a good-looking sales clerk says she is missing him already.

Thanking people is even more challenging. The straightforward British exchange "Thank you"—"Not at all" is strictly for beginners. Say a passerby asks you to change a dollar bill so she can make a phone call. You hand over four quarters. At this point, you risk embarking on a surreal conversation of the following kind—in the middle of the road:

Passerby: Thanks.
You: Not at all.
Passerby: You're welcome.
You: You're more than welcome.
Passerby: Sure.
You: Don't mention it.

In the more dramatic cases, the dialogue comes to an end in a dazzling display of "you're welcome" substitutes—"No prob-lem," "It's fine," "That's all right," "It's a pleasure," "Forget it," "It's nothing," "No sweat"—at the end of which it will be impos-sible to remember who was doing the thanking and who was be-ing thanked. The only answer in such cases is to walk off at a brisk pace. Unfortunately, it's not what you'd call an elegant solution.

• • •

IN THE EARLY nineteenth century, Americans began to shrug off the inferiority complex with respect to Great Britain that afflicted them in linguistic matters. Not that they spoke Oxford English before then. They spoke the way they felt like speaking, but they thought they were wrong. When the Scottish philosopher, David Hume, reproved Benjamin Franklin for using "colonize" and other Americanisms in a letter, Franklin apologized and promised not to do it again.

In contrast, by the early 1800s, the desire to do it their way had gained the upper hand. Americans began to invent new words (*self-made man*, *know-how*, and *businessman* in the sense of a person engaged in commerce) as well as adapting old words (*presidential*, *influential*). They shortened long words (*fanatic* became *fan*, *pantaloons* shrank to *pants*, and *gentlemen* to *gents*). Prepositions were added to verbs, changing their meaning (to *check in*, to *hold on*, and to *show off*). Some verbs became nouns (*dump*) and countless nouns became verbs. *To interview*, *to panic*, *to notice*, *to oppose*, and *to park* all date from the period.

The British have never forgiven the Americans. They have been complaining for the past hundred and fifty years. One of the first—and loudest—of those protesters was Charles Dickens, who claimed to have been shocked when a waiter asked him if he wanted to be served right away. As has since been noted, Dickens must have been particularly slow that day not to understand.

And yet for those who have learned their English in the British

Isles, the temptation to object—or worse, to be sarcastic—is strong. It must be resisted. American English has proved over the years that it has at least two qualities it can be proud of—immense creativity and an admirable tendency to simplify. If we Italians cannot understand what people are saying to us, then, as they say in these parts, it's our problem.

• • •

YOU DON'T NEED to be particularly astute, or to have the insight of a Thomas Jefferson ("The new circumstances under which we are placed, call for new words, new phrases, and for the transfer of old words to new objects"), to understand that America—and not Britain—is today the factory of the English language. Hollywood, and not Oxford, is teaching the language to the Chinese, the Russians, the Germans, and even the Italians, when they want to learn.

For those who love English, it is astounding to see how in America it is manhandled, masticated, chewed up, swallowed up, and spat back out again while retaining its charm and enhancing its functionality. The order of the day here is Shorten and Simplify (the reverse of Germany, where the motto is Elongate and Complicate). Why write *night*, *right*, and *light* when *nite*, *rite*, and *lite* are shorter, easier to remember, and closer to how you pronounce the words? Why should *although* (first recorded in 1275) not be brought up to date as *altho*? And why waste a vowel in *colour* and *honour* when *color* and *honor* will do just as well?

I admit that I am sometimes worried by the speed of these changes. The English I began to learn at fifteen so I could speak to the teenage girls on the promenade at Eastbourne (1972) is now the subject of scholarly treatises. Today, students at Georgetown—whose goal is still the same: getting off with girls—send round messages like this: VIPS RSVP ASAP, which means that very important people answer as soon as possible.

Novelties are not confined to the world of the young. This is one huge "free market of language" where the only criterion is how effective a word is. The proof of a term's value is its success. Large numbers of words from Yiddish have established themselves in everyday conversation, thanks to their expressiveness. Some of those to remember, on pain of ostracism from polite society, are:

chutzpah	impudence
schlock	poorly made
schmaltz	sentimentalism
to schmooze	to talk intimately
schmuck	an unpleasant individual

Computer terminals have long since taken on a life of their own, dialoguing in a newspeak that remains a mystery to me. One West Coast magazine offered its readers a series of words arranged in three columns. By taking one term from each, readers could create neologisms that mean anything or nothing (personally, I favor the latter view):

interactive	multimedia	suite
highspeed	server	architecture
network	e-mail	engine
revolutionary	reality	group
visionary	protocol	site
virtual	software	agent
web	chat	newsgroup
Mondo	communications	network

modem	parallel	CD-ROM
online	intelligent	agent
realtime	information	teleconference

Equally fascinating is the way numbers are used. They are potent, concise, immediately recognizable symbols so why only use them to do sums? That's what Americans think (actually, they don't think at all—they just do it). The number 2 often stands for the preposition *to* or the adverb *too*. The number 4 replaces *for*, 6 means *sex*, while 8 substitutes the syllable-*ate* in words such as *hate*, *fate*, or *late*. Then 9 is used in a Budweiser beer advertisement to form the adjective *canine*, which has become *K-9*. But the spiritual home of such experiments is the automobile license plate. The white Ferrari that belonged to Nicole Brown Simpson, the unfortunate, and now deceased, wife of O. J. Simpson, had the number plate L84AD8, or Late for a date. You will understand that nowadays you need sharp eyes and the brain of a crossword-puzzle addict to learn English in the United States.

Some innovations are even wilder, or more sophisticated. It depends on your point of view. American teenagers have learned to use their beepers—those little devices that tell you to call a telephone number—to send real messages. The numbers on the display should be read upside down so that they look like letters. A straightforward Hello is 07734 whereas 50538 represents the word *besos* (*kisses* in Spanish).

Experiments that would break a purist's heart—fortunately there aren't any purists in the United States, so there's no problem—are conducted with the letters of the alphabet. What counts is the pronunciation of each letter. X (pronounced *eks*) long ago replaced the word *extra* (as in X-Large). B has taken the place of the root form of the verb to be. R is used instead of *are* and U is commonly used in place of the second-person pronoun. In this way, "Are you happy?" becomes "R U happy?" For the same reason, a chain of toyshops is known as Toys R Us and the name of the biggest truck-rental company in the union is U Haul.

So much for the beginner's course. There are even bolder combinations. For example, the name of a used-car showroom, NU2U, reads "New to You," or the phrase You Can rendered in a cartoon by a drawing of a tin can with the letter U written on the front. Advertisements for the Washington subway carry the slogan, EZIN-EZOUT, to be translated "easy in, easy out." In other words, the name of the letter E, together with the American pronunciation of Z, is sufficient to indicate the adjective *easy*.

This taste—and talent—for initials is not new. The world-famous phrase *OK* has its origins in the United States. It is interesting to note that the Americans invented the expression, and then forgot why. The search for the derivation of *OK* has cost Allen Walker Read, a linguist from the University of Columbia, twenty years' work. Read discarded the following theories—the *OK* comes from the phrase Only Kissing, from Orrin Kendall cookies, the Haitian rum, Aux Cayes, the Greek expression, *ola kala* (everything's all right), from the Choctaw affirmation, *okeh*, or the native American chief, Old Keokuk—and established that the expression appeared for the first time in a Boston newspaper in 1839, as a lighthearted abbreviation of Oll Korrect. Acronyms were fashionable at the time and a Democratic OK Club was founded to support one politician's presidential campaign. A century and a half later, *OK* is the planet's most instantly recognizable expression. Italians as young as two get off the plane and spray their interlocutors with an indiscriminate hail of *OK*s, regardless of whether they actually agree with, or indeed understand, anything at all. The only part of the world where *OK* is relatively little used is the United States. The Americans are probably at this minute dreaming up some new expression they don't want to tell us about.

. . .

THE ONE THING Americans cannot do, or do badly, is spell. We won't go into the statistics, which are chilling (thirty million citizens are unable to read the label on a box of soap powder according to Literacy Volunteers of America). You only have to note the enthusiasm with which people follow the National Spelling Bee, an annual competition for schoolchildren from ten to fourteen years of age, to realize that America has one or two problems when it comes to writing words down correctly. The last edition was won by a student who spelled *proboscis* and *antediluvian* accurately, after the other finalists had fallen by the wayside over *lycanthrope*, *psalmodist*, and *pulverulent*. In all probability, students at any state middle school in Italy would be able spell these words properly.

But this, of course, is America. Here, children at elementary schools are invited to write using consonants only (the hated vowels, reason educationalists, have too uncertain a sound). Here, even more than in Great Britain, to be able to spell indicates culture, sophistication, and success in polite society. Not only that, the difficult words—the ones that torment schoolchildren and elicit admiration at parties—come mainly from Greek and Latin, two languages that flow in the veins of every European. But in South Carolina, these are not mere words. They are incantations.

When it comes to spelling, everyone gets it wrong all the time. The former vice president Dan Quayle showed that he didn't know how to write potato(e). The football star O. J. Simpson wrote after beating his wife that for what he had done there was no "ex-ceptible" (i.e., acceptable) excuse. And the wild man of Ameri-can letters, the journalist Hunter S. Thompson, once confessed to an interviewer that "weird" was one of the words he couldn't spell. ("Weird. And sheriff," he added.)

During the interminable "telephone war," AT&T launched an advertising campaign that urged Americans to dial 1-800-OPERA-TOR. MCI at once hit back by registering the 1-800-OPERATER number in the certain knowledge that many callers would get the spelling wrong and thus become their unwitting customers. I re-member my amazement when an American journalist asked me how to spell *maintenance*. Surprising, perhaps, but not unusual. Reporters and writers are spoiled by computers that automati-cally correct their mistakes, like those poor souls who can't mul-tiply sixteen by seven without a calculator. (Don't panic. The answer's one hundred and twelve.)

Spelling mistakes are so common that those who favor the present system are forced onto the defensive. The way words are written—they maintain—is a fascinating indication of how they were once pronounced. This view doesn't honestly sound like a winner with the millions of young Americans busy working out or wolfing Big Macs, whose intentions with regard to spelling are as ruthless as they are commendable. Their benchmark for the En-glish language is MTV Their arbiters, Beavis and Butthead (motto—"it sucks"). Prepare for the worst. It could be fun.

• • •

ON THE SUBJECT of spelling. In one of my earlier books, I men-tioned how in Great Britain, any Italian name more complicated than Rossi is liable to be distorted continuously. To prove my point, I listed twenty-six ways in which my surname had been misspelled. It was naïve of me. I didn't know at the time that I would be coming to the United States, where in six months they have reduced "Severgnini" to shreds.

Of course, since this is America, some people have tried to find explanations for my difficulties (apart from other people's obstinacy). According to AT&T Bell Laboratories, s is the most difficult sound to distinguish on the telephone because it involves high frequencies of between three and six thousand hertz while the telephone eliminates any distinction at more than four thousand. Other problem sounds are n, p, and b. As you will realize, I'm in trouble.

So, let's take a look at my spelling collection. Some combinations are masterpieces of anagrammatical imagination. I offer them for the reader's amusement, together with the name of the perpetrator (or artist, if you prefer).

We could begin with a few of the less culpable variations:

Mr. SEVIRGININI	(The Freedom Forum, Washington)
Mr. SEVIRGNINI	(AAA Potomac, Washington)
Mr. SEVERGNINE	(Georgetown University Hospital)
Mr. SEVERINI	(The Wyndham Hotel, New York)
Mr. SEVERIGNINI	(McLaughlin Group, Washington)
Mr. SEVERIGNINNI	(The Studio Theatre, Washington)
Mr. SEVERIGHIMI	(Brooks Brothers, Washington)
Mr. SEVERIGNI	(The Economist Distribution Center, Lakewood, N.J.)

There is the inevitable:

GUISEPPE SEVERGNINI	(American Express, and dozens of others)

which is a ritual American punishment for anyone whose name contains the diphthong *iu*. It happens to everyone. A few days ago, the former president George Bush was presenting Rudy Giuliani, the mayor of New York, and called him Guiliani. The magazine *Washington Life* said that Guiliano Amato was the Italian head of state, inverting the order of the vowels, getting the job wrong, and letting everyone know it was two prime ministers out of date.

Then there is an intriguing:

BEPPE SEVERGNIA	(Office of the European Commission Delegation, Washington)

an embarrassing

Mr. SEDERINI (little bottoms)	(MCI telephone company)

and four minor masterpieces:

GIUSUPPE SSEVERGNINI	(United Airlines)
BETTY SEVEGNINI	(World Press Review)
BEPPE SEVERGNINY	(Institute for International Studies)
BEPE VERGNINI	(Federal Communications Commission)

Some contributors preferred to concentrate on the first name:

BERRE SEVERGNINI	(Olsson's Books, Washington)
BEPPO SEVERGNINI	(National Press Club, Washington)
GIUETTE SEVERGNINI	(Pacific Agency, Seattle)

GIUSETTE SEVERGNINI	(Sheraton Manhattan, New York)
GUISSEPPEE SEVERGNINI	(Georgetown Basket, Washington)
GIUSPPE SEVERGNINI	(Arthur Andersen, New York)
GEORGE SEVERGNINI	(Greyhound Lines Inc., Dallas)

There was one consolation. I've always thought that my wife's name, Ortensia Marazzi, was relatively easy to master, as well as being attractive. But

ORTENSIU MAROZZI	(American Automobile Association, Washington)

is much more entertaining.

• • •

IT'S NOT DIFFICULT to sympathize with how some Italians speak English. You've only got to see what Americans do to Italian.

If the language of Dante, which so many profess to esteem, could sue its admirers for harassment, it would be a multibillion-aire. I'm not talking about the mistakes made by well-intentioned learners, or errors committed by Italian Americans who are forgetting their mother tongue. These are legitimate, and even engaging, cases. What annoys me is all the rest—misquotations, wrongly transcribed names, and a complete lack of interest for Italian spelling, which has none of the insidious traps of English.

Over the past few months, I've been keeping a scrapbook of cuttings to convince myself that I haven't been imagining things. A few examples? There was an article in the *New York Times* by a writer who had been robbed on the *autostrada*. To distract him, the criminals had pointed at their car and said *Quasto!*, with a *q*. I don't think so. They may have been crooks but they probably weren't entirely illiterate. "Broken down" in Italian is *guasto* with a *g*. In the *New York Times* again, Silvio Berlusconi was referred to twice as *Il Azzurro* instead of *L'Azzurro*, while in the *Washington Post*, the excellent Mary McGrory has described how she was in Italy when the Watergate scandal broke out. The Italian headlines she quotes are wrong (*Cox lizenziato*—instead of *licenziato*—*da Nixon*) as are the conversations she recalls (*A ceduto le bobbine* instead of *Ha ceduto le bobine*), unless perhaps Ms. McGrory was trying to reproduce the pronunciation of a Roman taxi driver.

Let's move on from the press to real life. Very few of the restaurants in America take the trouble to check the spelling of the dishes they offer. I conserve as if it were the relic of a saint the menu from the Café Lombardy—my first meal in America this time round—for it includes *Misto delle Caseine* (presumably *delle Cascine*, indicating a farmhouse grill rather than a mixture of soluble milk proteins), *Agnoloti Carvella* (the first word has a *t* missing, the second is a complete mystery), and *Pasta 'd Gornio* and *Zuppa 'd Gornio* (which should be *del giorno*, I suppose, like the French *du jour*; the apostrophe is also incorrect).

When they're not mistreating our language, Americans take it out on our nationality for they even manage to get the word *Italians* wrong. In the twenties, many people said Aitalians instead of Italians, thinking that the first vowel was pronounced the same way as *idea* or *iron*. Nothing has changed. And it's not just the trucker from Kansas—who would need a week to find Italy on a map—who has problems. Presidents get it wrong, too. The weekly magazine *The New Yorker* tells the story of how Jimmy

Carter, introducing the governor of New York, Mario Cuomo, at a Democratic convention, called him an Eye-talian. Perhaps it's better that way. Any illusion we might have that Italy counts for something in this world is quickly crushed. In the twinkling of an Eye (-talian).

November

*I*n Italy, neighborhoods have squares. In America, they have supermarkets. And in Georgetown, the hub of neighborhood life is the local Safeway. This huge store—it's on your right as you go up Wisconsin Avenue—is also known as Social Safeway because (so they say, I hasten to add) it's a good place for a casual romantic encounter. Legend has it that on Friday evenings, a cart abandoned in the aisles means a new couple has been formed. He and she (or he and he, or she and she) have hit it off and left Safeway together, piling all their shopping into one cart.

I have to admit that I have never found this story very convincing. In seven months, the most erotic things I have seen in the store were the oven-ready turkey legs at Thanksgiving. But I will admit that Social Safeway is a civilized place. For there is also a Soviet Safeway in one of the poorer areas on the east side of town, which is decidedly less genteel. At Social Safeway, they say you can bump into Hillary Rodham Clinton (I've never seen her) but at Soviet Safeway, you're more likely to find yourself facing a gang of unpleasantly aggressive adolescents. At Social, the greens swell with pride and the beef is a healthy pink. At Soviet, the meat and vegetables look as if they have been sold on by an out-of-town diner that couldn't find any takers.

Yet whatever their social status, American supermarkets—which are the genuine article because the term was coined here in the twenties—induce a feeling of bewilderment in European visitors. Despite the fact that we have been used to abundance for forty years, the range of goods on offer leaves us speechless and open-mouthed. It is shocking to find, for example, an incredible variety of fundamentally superfluous products like breakfast cereals, whose 220 different combinations of shapes, ingredients, and vitamins look sinfully self-indulgent. It might be that unless Americans can choose from fifteen versions of the same product, they will think rationing has been introduced.

Personally, I don't think I'll ever get used to it. The average consumer, according to statistics, makes fourteen impulse purchases each time he or she goes to a supermarket. I seem to make nothing but such acquisitions, only to regret them immediately afterward. Sometimes they are translucent substances with iridescent colors and names that begin with Jell-O. On other occasions, they are variations on familiar products, such as potato chips flavored with cheese and onions, or similar perversions. And of course, I also fall victim to homesickness. That's the only excuse I can offer for buying the Milano biscuits whose packaging bore this unlikely suggestion: "Imagine you are strolling down the cobbled street to your favorite European bakery. The aroma of the Old World fills the air . . ."

I am not put off even by names that should be enough to warn you on their own. They are generally extremely long and hard to pronounce (short names like Mars or 7-UP are used for export products). How can you trust a margarine that calls itself I Can't

Believe It's Not Butter? What on earth is a Cheez Whiz Zap-A-Pak, apart from some sort of curd-based concoction? And what about Devil's Food Cookies? Would you give your children half a kilo of Trail Mix, a perfidious farrago of savory crackers, cookies, pieces of chocolate, and marshmallow? Americans do.

And what about the packaging? Everything, from potato chips to paper napkins, is sold in (extended) family-size packs. What if you don't have an extended family? That's your problem. The word *wholesale* stimulates salivation in the average American and the phrase "25 percent more" triggers off the hoarding instinct. I have tried to point out to the woman at the checkout in Safeway that no one, unless they are suffering from some sort of neurosis, can possibly consume five thousand paper napkins in less than a year. She gave me a bored look and said, "Throw away the ones you don't use."

It is hard for non-Americans to understand that behind all these exotic labels lies a solid traditionalism. When it comes to food products, Americans are conservatives. In many market segments, the leading brand is the same as it was in 1925—Kellogg's in breakfast cereals, Campbell in soups, Del Monte in tinned fruit, Nabisco for cookies, and Wrigley for chewing gum. The nation's favorite foods have not changed. These include that hideous invention, peanut butter, and "fresh" chicken that has just come out of the freezer. (Prod one. You could go bowling with it.)

And that's where the real difficulty lies—penetrating the country's food-related mythology. Few are aware, for example, that the merest glimpse of a can of Spam sets American gastric juices flowing. Spam—so they tell me—is not just a food product. It's an entire subculture. Since its introduction in 1937, five billion tins have been sold. There are Spam cookbooks, Spam-flavored ice cream, Spam sculptures, Spam T-shirts, Spam clubs, and Spam festivals. Spam served the nation in the Second World War and in

135

the Korean War. It is commemorated on car license plates (MMM-SPAM). It has inspired poets. What, if not true love, could have prompted Jack Collom (from Boulder, Colorado) to compose the following acrostic?

Somehow the texture, out of nowhere,
Produces a species of
Atavistic anomie, a
Melancholy memory of food.

• • •

THIS MORNING, THERE was a leaflet in my newspaper suggesting I should take out a subscription to the *Nutrition Action Healthletter*. For the modest sum of ten dollars, this publication offers to transform every meal into an angstfest. It offers life-saving information and lists ten "Foods You Should Never Eat," including Quaker 100% Natural Cereal, Kung Pao Chicken, Fettuccini Alfredo, and Dunkin' Donuts Cake Doughnut. Quite apart from the fact that your correspondent would never put anything called a Dunkin' Donuts Cake Doughnut into his mouth, I begin to wonder if the Americans have perhaps gone too far.

I sometimes suspect that gastronomic masochism is a game, and that the only people who take it seriously are we foreigners. This is how you play. You choose a particularly well-loved food and then you wait for the referee to tell you it is bad for you (the referees can be newspapers, radio, television, or the *Nutrition Action Healthletter*). This goes on during the week. On Saturday, everyone rushes to stock up on alternatives, then on Monday you start looking for a new food threat.

All this means that the list of banned foods is long and new names are constantly being added. Recently, it was the turn of popcorn and Coca-Cola. Poor old popcorn suffered an attack that not even Baghdad was subjected to at the height of the Gulf War. The first wave came from the Center for Science in the Public Interest (CSPI), which called popcorn a nutritional disaster and the Godzilla of snacks. According to the CSPI, one portion of popcorn contains more saturated fats than a fast food meal. If you add butter, then the fat content is tripled. A medium-size bucket (medium-size for Americans, mammoth for us) with about twenty-five handfuls is the equivalent of a bacon-and-egg breakfast, plus a Big Mac, plus fries, plus a steak with the trimmings (all of which, of course, are delicious).

Coca-Cola got off more lightly but is nonetheless on the defensive. The charge this time was that it has too low a food content. The attack was launched by the president of the Senate agriculture committee, who presented a bill to encourage schools to ban the sale of drinks with minimal nutritional value. This proposal, it goes without saying, was not welcomed by the Coca-Cola Company, which asked schools to lobby against it and reminded them that their cut on sales from automatic vending machines helps to pay for school sports, publications, bands, and uniforms.

These are the events behind the food controversy of the century, at least for the next month. It shouldn't last any longer than that. Not only are other foods lining up impatiently to take their place in the dock, and get their well-earned fifteen minutes of fame, but it also looks unlikely that the march toward a healthier table will be able to ignore a number of (well-protected) minorities. Children, for example, adore popcorn and Coca-Cola, and are far less neurotic than their parents. Cinemagoers can't concentrate on the film without a bucket of popcorn in their lap. And then there are the Europeans. If they won't let us play with real junk food, why should we come to the States in the first place?

• • •

ONE OF THE favorite topics of conversation with Europeans in
America is how big people are. Transatlantic obesity is a contin-
ual source of wonder. The American *didietro*, or bottom (one of
the many ways of referring to the appurtenance in question), has
a hypnotic and vaguely soothing, effect on foreigners. If that's the
price for being the world's number-one nation, then no thanks.

Just this once, the myth is not tourist-inspired. It's actually
true. Journalists, sociologists, and doctors—in that order—are
studying the phenomenon with an interest that borders on obsession. The finding that set off the latest alarm (not for the first time,
and certainly not for the last) was published by the Centers for
Disease Control—the proportion of Americans who are fat (i.e., at
least 20 percent overweight) has increased in a few years from
one quarter of the population to one third. Obese teenagers ac-
counted for 15 percent of the total during the seventies. Today,
they make up 21 percent. There has been a rise of four pounds
(1.8 kg) for men and nine pounds (4 kg) for women in average
weight among thirty- to thirty-nine-year-olds. Over the coming
Christmas holidays, Americans will put on an average of five and
a half pounds (2.5 kg). In the United States, January and February are traditionally devoted to remorse and gymnastics.

I could go on filling the page with figures but it would be superfluous. You don't need statistics to see that this is a Big Country. Just take a walk through any mall. Happy smiling couples
clutching doughnuts that resemble truck tires fill the corridors.
Literally. Groups of enormous women in distressingly taut leg-
gings devour ice creams the size of wedding cakes. There's a kind
of cheerful "Who cares?" attitude about them that should not,
however, deceive. Obese Americans, like fat people everywhere,
don't generally have a great time.

One further aspect is less obvious. Obesity is associated with economic status. It's not just poor people who get fat. But poor people get fat more. The group that has the highest proportion of overweight individuals in absolute terms is African American women. Half of those stunning sixteen-year-olds who are now strutting their stuff round America will have a very different way of walking and size of jeans in a few years' time. Fat has become the ultimate stigma of failure. Money melts away even the most tenacious adipose tissue.

All attempts to find a solution—the society-wide obsession with the fat-free road to food paradise—have proved to be not only useless but actually counterproductive. When Americans discover that a food has only half the fat content, they eat three times as much as they normally would. And they eat everywhere, without interruption or inhibition. The self-indulgence that enables the nation to shop until it drops also tempts it to grab any forbidden treat that lies to hand. "These are the Satisfied States of America," commented the Czech writer Bohumil Hrabal after his first visit.

The phenomenon has been named compulsive recreational eating and the manufacturers pander to it by soothing the consumer's guilty conscience. On the one hand, they make the king-sizes, extra-larges, super-sizes, and double-gulps even bigger than before and, on the other, their marketing staff invent even more reassuring slogans. One snack with a worrying name (Frito-Lays New Baked Tostitos) carries this advertising copy—"Thanks to our chips you can allow yourself more snacking fun! Great taste, no guilt!" Some efforts have been made to stem this tide, but it's always too little and too late. The Georgetown Safeway—showing that its ideals are as high as its prices—has opened a candy-free checkout so that customers won't be tempted as they wait in line to pay.

The other day I went with a French friend to a university basketball match at the U.S. Air Arena in Landover. The people sitting next to us—indeed, all our neighbors—appeared to be suffering from St. Vitus's dance. At any time, at least two of them were getting up to go and get huge packs of popcorn, hot dogs, pizzas, rolls, syrup-drenched waffles, ice creams, hamburgers, or baked potatoes smothered in cheese. My companion, her mind drifting nostalgically off to the restaurants of her native Provence, was nauseated. This Italian was left speechless. I would have liked to shout something terribly banal along the lines of "Please don't eat between meals!" But I would have regretted it. Putting on weight and then grumbling about being too fat is a fundamental human right in this country.

• • •

ANYONE WHO THINKS that serious shopping is for well-heeled ladies of leisure should come to America. A pre-Christmas mall would tempt a desert-dwelling ascetic (indeed, an ascetic would be especially vulnerable). It's not just the quality of the merchandise that attracts. It's the prices, the presentation, the special offers, and a moral atmosphere that has already forgiven you before you've even thought about sinning.

Shopping in America is one big party, and never let it be said that an Italian refused an invitation to a party. I honestly thought I was strong enough to resist the siren song of any shop window but after one or two embarrassing episodes (my credit card statement still bears the scars), I reached the following conclusion. Shopping U.S.-style is to its Italian counterpart what a cruise missile is to a slingshot—much more sophisticated and infinitely more dangerous.

But there's also an ironic side to the question because the inventors of modern shopping were the Europeans, not the Americans. While shoppers in Milan were strolling in the Galleria Vittorio Emanuele and Londoners inspected the windows of Burlington Arcade, Americans were still chasing their longer established native counterparts around on horseback. When it arrived in the United States during the thirties thanks to a Viennese immigrant called Victor Gruen, the shopping center was intended to re-create the city center-with-shops of European capitals. The word *mall* itself only became firmly established at the end of the sixties. The name derives from a seventeenth-century Italian game known in English as pall-mall, a forerunner of croquet that involved hitting a ball along a court with a stick.

But despite having invented the concept, we are still defenseless before American-style shopping. Take special offers, which in Italy are often not very special and sometimes don't even deserve the name *offer*. Sales in the United States are plastic-bustingly genuine. A few days ago, I took two friends to the Macy's at Tyson's Corner (one of Washington's commercial satellites). On that particular day, everything—from cookies to fitted kitchens—was being sold at a 40 percent discount. Many articles were reduced by a further 20 percent. My friends had coupons that entitled them to another 20 percent off. The result was that a pair of hundred-dollar Timberland ankle boots, after adding up all the discounts, worked out at eight dollars. I know of no Italian who can resist temptations of this magnitude.

Another means of overcoming the consumer's psychological defenses—such as they are—is pricing. In America, you will never see an article that costs ten dollars ($10.00). They always cost nine dollars ninety-nine ($9.99). The reason for this curious practice is not to break down customer resistance by convincing them that they are spending nine dollars rather than ten (that came later). Originally, shopkeepers avoided round figures to prevent assistants from slipping money into their own pockets. They had to give the shopper a penny in change and so were forced to open the till, a noisy operation executed to the accompaniment of bells and the rattle of cash drawers.

A second point in favor of American shopping is that the sales assistants genuinely want to sell, and triumphantly succeed in doing so. They don't behave as if you have interrupted them, the way their colleagues in Europe tend to. The old excuse that "We haven't got your size/color/model" simply doesn't exist in the States. The assistant—whether working on commission or out of loyalty to the company—will always find what it was you were looking for. Competition among the various retail groups is based on these details, as well as on price and quality. Sales technique, parking facilities, and restrooms (including the softness of the toilet paper—the newspapers compile top-ten charts) all count, too. Consumers are like the grouse on a Scottish estate. The question is not whether they will be shot, but who is going to bag them.

It has been mooted that this system, whereby everyone acquires whatever they want as soon as it crosses their mind to do so in a huge carnival of self-indulgence, could suffer a crisis when America's wardrobes are finally full. One day there will be no more space for the residue of yesterday's enthusiasms (golf clubs, dark rooms, skiing jackets and boots, gadgets, and manuals that tell you what the gadgets are for). But frankly, I doubt it. The closets of this land, as we have noted, are extremely capacious.

We now come to the third thing in favor of American sales staff (and the umpteenth weak point of their European colleagues). Almost all shops, and all department stores, have adopted the so-called liberal return policy. In practice, this means that any purchase can be returned after it has been sold, without question. Legend has it that the Nordstrom department store once took a car tire back, even though they don't sell tires.

Italian eyes light up when these stories are told. The return policy in American stores opens up infinite possibilities. Children could have bicycles, skateboards, or computers, keep them for a while, and then hand them back when the new model comes out. Middle-aged female purchase-and-return pros would be able to pick up an evening dress on Friday and take it back on Monday. Rubber dinghies and swimwear would be bought in June and taken back in September, in an exciting new form of cost-free rental.

Curiously, Americans rarely seem to take advantage of the system. The same goes for European residents. ("Everyday life in America is a potent solvent," as someone once said.) Assistants who don't stare at us as if we were terrorists when we ask to exchange an article automatically win our approval. Cash desks that open to return our purchase price inspire eulogies. In fact, the only people who take advantage of the liberal return policy are the very people who ought, in theory, to be its victims—the storekeepers. When the customer knows that goods can be returned, inhibitions disappear and turnover increases. Moral—the liberal return policy should be banned by the United Nations, like chemical weaponry. We traveling Italians would feel a lot safer.

• • •

THE BIG DEPARTMENT stores (Macy's, Hechts, Sears, Nordstrom) are not the only ones to deprive us of our free will. The

"There it is. It's cheap. I'll buy it" trap is also laid in specialist stores (Home Depot, Staples), ordinary retail outlets, and even corner shops.

Our now familiar Thirty-fourth Street has one of these mom-and-pop stores at the junction with Dent Place. Distant relations of an Italian *drogheria*, these establishments are open around the clock, are visible from a distance, and sell everything from milk to newspapers, wine, lightbulbs, bread, and lip gloss. Frequently, they are the first refuge of Asian immigrants (who do the selling) or of Europeans (who buy) for they offer a rare opportunity to shop in a cosy environment, where there is a real face behind the counter, without having to get the car out.

The posters and neon signs in the window tell you what's on sale.

Cold Beer

Coca-Cola

GROCERIES

Snacks

MILK

Newspapers

MANGO MADNESS

In this list, there is all of America. As much, and perhaps more, than can be found in the marble of the Lincoln Memorial. There is simplicity, self-reliance, practicality, and the urge to squirrel away stocks of food. These are values that we Europeans struggle to understand. And yet we sense somehow that the red neon signs in the dark are America's art. It's an unintentional art form and the best—some say the only—kind that this land has produced. We gaze in silent admiration, as is right.

• • •

IN THE STATES, discounts are not a way of paying less. They are your entry tickets to a world in which Americans are entirely at home while foreign residents can only gasp in wonder as they veer from moments of wild enthusiasm to black depression. Beyond all doubt, new arrivals in America ought to be given discount induction courses, just as English courses are available for those who do not know the language. After the first ten lessons, the student will realize that American discounts have little in common with a *sconto* in Italy. The Italian *sconto* is an unofficial favor, granted to an individual, that allows the seller to look generous and the buyer to feel important. In America, discounts are scientific. If you are entitled, you get one. Otherwise, nothing doing. The problem, of course, is to know when you are entitled to a discount.

For example, let's take booking a hotel. There is no fixed rate as such. There is, instead, a whole range of prices tucked away inside the computer of the duty clerk, who will do his or her best not to reveal them. If you pay in a certain way, that might get you a lower rate. Being a member of a club, association, group, or other organization could earn you a bigger discount. A credit card could get you an upgrade to a better room. And if you have flown with a certain airline, booked from abroad, or mentioned a special offer published in a particular newspaper (which tells you in a conspiratorial whisper to "call this number and ask for XACT"), that, too, could clinch a special tariff. If you are not entitled to any of these reductions (mainly because you are unaware of their existence), and the duty clerk takes pity, you'll be offered a discretionary discount, which is the U.S. equivalent of a *sconto*.

The business of coupons is rather more complicated. Do you remember those bits of colored paper that ask you to cut along the dotted line? In Italy, their brief careers end in the wastepaper basket. In America, they open the door to a wonderland.

There are ten pages of coupons at the front of the telephone Yellow Pages and Green Pages (yes, they have green ones as well as yellow ones) and they entitle you to reductions on everything from eyewear to immigration consultancy. The newspapers carry swathes of coupons. At some sales, they are distributed to the gatecrashers who queue up at seven in the morning. Discount professionals can be recognized by their coupon-organizers, little folders in which apparently normal citizens keep their unused coupons.

That's the beginner's course. Then there are coupons you can use at the sales. Coupons for club members. Manufacturer's coupons and coupons tied in with airline advertising campaigns. Some bars have special offers for people who hand over a certain coupon. Sometimes (not always) there's a catch, or the conditions are impossibly complicated. This is a coupon issued by the Sir Walter Raleigh restaurant, which appeared in the *Week-End* supplement of the *Washington Post*:

$10.00 discount

For one dinner during the month of your birthday. With this coupon, minimum two people, one coupon per couple. Each person must purchase an entrée to the value of $13.95 (or more). The $10.00 discount applies only to individual celebrating birthday. Proof of birthdate required (driver's license, etc.). No age minimum. Not valid with other discounts, promotions, or Early Bird Specials. Expires 14 December.

This legalistic, pedantic prose would convince most Europeans to dine elsewhere. Americans, however, love this kind of coupon because it allows them to show off their competence. Here are the four basic rules, of which newcomers are generally unaware and which they would be well-advised to learn by heart:

1. No discount is easy to understand. Like matrimony and mountaineering, shopping has to offer new challenges.

2. No discount is too generous. If it was such a great deal, they wouldn't be offering it to you.

3. No discount is too little. If a triangle of paper will get twenty-five cents off razor blades, then hand it over. Americans aren't ashamed, so why should you be?

4. Foreigners are there to pay the full price so that Americans can work out how much they have saved.

It is sometimes, I must admit, impossible to resist the hypnotic attraction of the coupons. The only people who might elude their mortal embrace are those who throw away the coupon sections so skilfully interleaved with their Sunday papers to look like bonafide supplements. When envelopes brimming with discounts and promises flop onto the doormat under the letterbox, you have to be strong. Don't open them. That was what got Aladdin into trouble. Once the genie gets out of the lamp, you don't know where it's all going to end.

The coupon's natural ally in this environment is the catalog. The original mail-order catalog was printed in a Chicago attic in 1872 on a single sheet of paper. Today, there are thousands of them, intent on hustling the most appalling wares. In the past week, as I have been writing these pages, catalogs and coupons have been sliding through the door—Christmas is coming—and spreading through the house like unpleasant gremlins. I think there are five or six pounds of the things squeezed into chubby envelopes with names like *Money Mailer* and *Value Pack*.

One hundred grams of envelope (a little under four ounces) contain: one free gourmet pizza (free pizzas are always of the gourmet variety); address stickers in the shape of the state where you live (five hundred for $4.99); thirty-six static-energy Christmas decals ($12; store price $26); a china plate with the words "The Year of the Wolf" ($29.50); a dental checkup, oral hygiene, and two X-rays (courtesy of Nancy and Cecilia, $29); Jiffi Maid professional domestic services ($10 discount); repairs (Epic Construction, $500 discount); chimney-sweeps (Kick Ash); ten sunlamp sessions for $45; Chanel No. 5 perfume for $2 (the small print tells you it's only imitation Chanel); one hundred personalized pencils; a belt-bag with your initials in gold plate; and a cartoon in which the characters' faces can be replaced with those of your family ($19.95). Finally, for just two dollars, you can purchase 180 specialist catalogs (selling everything from kites to removable tattoos), each of which contains hundreds of coupons, samples and . . . offers for more catalogs. This is the marketing equivalent of a black hole. Once you have fallen into its grasp, there's no escape.

December

*H*olidays in the States are the totem poles around which a contented tribe performs its ritual dances. There's one on Independence Day, Fourth of July (which, from an emotional point of view, is worth twenty of our Second of June Republic Days). And another at the pagan festival of Halloween. Then there's Thanksgiving Day (we don't say thanks in Italy—if we're satisfied, we merely refrain from complaining). And, of course, there is Christmas.

The traditional celebrations that sometimes weigh uncomfortably on European shoulders are celebrated in America as conquests. Having a tradition means having a past. And when you have a past, you have some basic certainties. New arrivals, whether they are Koreans who have come to stay or Italians who just want to look around, are immediately won over by the atmosphere. On their first Halloween, with its disguises, the ghosts and children tricking or treating, they feel vaguely silly. When their second comes around, they're veterans, keen to tell the next generation of newcomers what to do.

At Christmas, we Europeans ought to be better prepared, at

least in theory. But that's not the case. First of all, the pre-Christmas period in America is endless. It starts the day after Thanksgiving, which is on the fourth Thursday in November. From then on, the country's progress toward December 25 is awesome in its military precision, organization, and sheer scale.

At a stroke, the appeal of the festively illuminated malls becomes irresistible. Not to go shopping is considered more than merely eccentric. It's as profoundly un-American as actually walking in town or removing the ice from your Coca-Cola. Television stations and newspapers vie with each other to find the most Christmassy stories. Do-gooders are at a premium, and can name their own price. Christmas movies, filmed in July by profusely sweating Santas, finally hit the cinemas. Commercial premises of all kinds, from parking lots to funeral parlors, put up decorations and enthusiasm reaches such a peak that African Americans have introduced, to coincide with Christmas, the ancient festival of Kwanzaa, which dates as far back as 1966, and is totally unheard-of in Africa.

Like a huge, powerful limousine, America majestically gets into gear. It trots out its well-loved seasonal clichés and lays out its Yuletide stall. Ten thousand different catalogs distribute hundreds of millions of copies and several billion greetings cards jam the postal service, which is not noted for its efficiency at the best of times. The letterbox begins to fill up with the business cards of impromptu purveyors of fragrant and realistic trees and firewood. These entrepreneurs are generally a couple of suspicious-looking individuals with checked shirts and woolly hats who clamber out of a pickup with West Virginia plates. They must split their sides laughing on the way home to think that some people—us—will pay a dollar for a lump of firewood.

And yet there is nothing vulgar or irritating about the way in which the religious feast is transformed into a festival. The American Christmas has lost its Anglo-Saxon roots and become a popular celebration, where the religion is noble feelings, the only ones that can unite people of such different faiths, or of no faith at all. Crowded malls, overworked credit cards, and overloaded tables are not a betrayal of the feast. They are the feast. In a certain sense, the provincial Italy of traditional sweetmeats like *pandoro* is more hypocritical. All it takes for an almost entirely Catholic nation to forget the awe-inspiring splendor of what happened that first Christmas Day is a few presents, a slice of cake, and a bottle of spumante wine.

• • •

DECEMBER IS THE season of get-togethers. There is no office, company, or association that doesn't have a Christmas party, where colleagues who have hated each other all year are forced to pretend they are friends. In Italy, we are more serious from that point of view. If we detest someone, we don't take time off.

These parties are an excellent vantage point from which to observe the behavior patterns of the American citizenry. Not the trendsetters, but what we might call the silent majority, if it would just shut up for a minute. When you see a fad or an attitude at a Christmas party, it means that America has chewed it up, digested it, and painted the Stars and Stripes on the front. That's when you've got to start taking it seriously.

At the parties I have been to, for example, the rules were— bizarre drinks, low-fat food, and no smoking. It's easy to predict that smokers in the United States are about to suffer the same fate as the Native Americans—annihilation. The last few tribes, with their pathetic Bic lighters, are already confined to special reservations in most foul-smelling hotel rooms, in the restaurant no-man's-land that lies between the kitchen and the restroom, and in the back-row seats of airplanes where the cabin staff's discretionary cosmetic fragrances mingle with the pungent aroma of reheated chicken. These unfortunates pass the time as best they can—sending each other smoke signals.

Here's what they'll tell you in America if you ask for anyone's opinion on the antismoking laws. They'll say that those laws are like stagecoaches or typewriters: antiques. Americans have already done—and undone—everything there is to do on the subject, passing decrees and bans, taking legal action against the bans, making criminal charges and holding trials. The final verdict is—there shall be no smoking. Lighting up at table in the States isn't impolite. It's an act of aggression. You'd be better off trying to blow your nose on the tablecloth, drink from the finger bowl, or stare openly down your hostess's cleavage. You're more likely to get away with it.

In the face of this apartheid, the tobacco industry has reacted with quite incredible chutzpah, even though their conscience is far from clear (when they found out about the effects of smoking, they kept the results secret). Now the manufacturers say they want to defend human rights. In this battle of the hypocrites, the casualties are of course those people who smoke three cigarettes a day and get treated like terrorists if they admit they have a packet in the house.

Finding out whether it is acceptable to smoke on any given occasion has become a delicate exercise. Take this nonsmoker's word for it. The No Smoking signs are disappearing, like the ones that used to say No Spitting. Who could possibly think of doing anything so inelegant? For some time now, there have been signs saying, Smoking Permitted (but only if you ask, politely, on bended knee). At private dinner parties, you can spot the smokers straight away. After the coffee has been served, they look round furtively for an accomplice or an ashtray.

All things considered, there are fewer problems in public areas where at least the rules are clear. In schools, if there is a wisp of smoke coming out of a window, the fire service arrives in a flash. For a teacher, lighting up a cigarette in front of the students is more serious than bringing a bazooka into class, which might actually be useful for keeping discipline. Nowadays, it is the teaching staff that nips out for a smoke behind the bike sheds, once the preserve of rebellious adolescents. And in restaurants, they'll ask you simply, "Smoking or non?" You're supposed to say, "Non," as if it was not quite nice to repeat the hideous S-word.

• • •

ITALIANS DON'T COPY the important things about America, such as patriotism, optimism, and a sense of personal responsibility. Our passion, which is shared by three-quarters of the world's population, is to imitate the superficial aspects of American life, which include vocabulary, soft drinks, jeans, hairstyles, films, and songs.

While America was turning out genuine novelties, we could pretend that we got there second, which is not so bad. We countered Elvis with Little Tony. Levi's were challenged by Carrera jeans, and Harley-Davidson bikes by Ducati. The Italian answer to Coca-Cola was Royal-Cola and our Marilyn Monroe was, for want of anyone better, Sandra Milo. Now that Americans have started imitating and are revamping, rediscovering, or redesigning, Italy is forced to copy copiers. That's the bad news. The good news is that we haven't realized we're doing it yet.

Here's some proof. This year's big musical event was Woodstock, a shameless piece of recycling that produced the weird phenomenon of young people pretending to be middle-aged and oldsters—sorry, parents—deluding themselves that they were young again. Other episodes over which rivers of ink—and the odd tear—have been spilled were the comebacks staged by Barbra Streisand and the Rolling Stones. Class acts, sure enough, but not exactly cutting edge.

The most successful film has been *The Flintstones*, a celluloid version of the old Hanna & Barbera cartoon strip, and *Forrest Gump*, a breathtakingly ambitious exercise in nostalgia—forty years of American history in 140 minutes on-screen. The book on which the film is based, and the record of the sound track, top the best-seller lists, and the songs that accompany Gump's personal odyssey range from the Beach Boys to the Doors, from "California Dreamin' " to "Sweet Home Alabama." If you come over to the States, that's what people are listening to at every traffic light, in every bar, and in every living room. The new stuff—Seattle grunge or L.A. new sound—is for German or Italian tourists, or anyone else who isn't too picky.

Television has been taken over by the Power Rangers, a gang of teenagers with superpowers who are almost endearingly uncomplicated. Batman and Nembo Kid were postmodern enigmas in comparison. The X-Men, superheroes with wings, masks, and colored capes who first appeared in 1963, have also become cult figures. And "The Brady Bunch," a high-saccharine-content TV series from the seventies, is also due to make a comeback. In addition to reruns of the original episodes, there are plans for a full-length film with new actors.

And that's not all. The star of the current literary scene, Cormac McCarthy, echoes Faulkner. Bill Clinton takes his inspiration from John Kennedy (flamboyance, women, and all). In fashion, forties-style underwear, flannels from the fifties, jackets from the sixties, and maxi-skirts from the seventies have all been revived. In New York, where they're always one step ahead (or, in this case, behind), old-fashioned narrow suspenders are back, as well as—are you ready for this?—women's corsets.

We could go on but I think I have made my point. America has started imitating itself, or rather, it is ransacking the lumber-room of its recent past, and we Italians are destined to ape America. If nations were produced like *Rambo* films, then this would no longer be the United States of America. It would be "U.S.A. 2—The Comeback." And us? Perhaps "Italy 3—The Eternal Pursuit."

• • •

QUESTION: WHAT CURIOUS connection do Marlon Brando, Barbie, yuppies, D day, and Woodstock have with Hiroshima? No. Not the noise level. Or Donald Duck with chewing gum and the moon? Simple. They have all celebrated, or are about to celebrate, a birthday, whether it's their seventieth (Brando), sixtieth (Donald Duck), fiftieth (D day and Hiroshima), thirty-fifth (Barbie), twenty-fifth (Woodstock and the moon landing), or tenth (yuppies). The oldest of the bunch is chewing gum (125th). Which may not be without some deeper significance.

The anniversary bug, I suspect, has hit America hard. It's a sort of Prozac with no side effects apart from a certain monotony. There's nothing wrong with respect for the past, except when it turns into an obsession. The time that passes between an event and its celebration is contracting alarmingly. You don't have to wait a hundred years to commemorate something anymore. Twenty-five is long enough, or ten, or five, or even three. In the case of celebrities, the demise of the individual concerned is no longer a prerequisite. Marlon Brando's seventieth birthday, for example, was greeted with fireworks by the autumn publishing campaigns.

There is definitely a sentimental side to this orgy of commemoration. A generation of tenderhearted forty-somethings seems determined to re-create, review, and reassess the past. Often (if it is at all possible to make a buck by doing so), the anniversary is accompanied by a new version of the event, as was the case with Woodstock. When a physical celebration is more difficult to stage, as with Neil Armstrong's moonwalk, then the nation is subjected to a barrage of TV shows, magazine covers, articles, interviews, and comments.

In some cases, the anniversary is an opportunity to reflect on the past. D day celebrations went some way toward making the horrors and heroism of the Second World War better known. Yet in the end, they were transformed into an orgy of nostalgia, in which anyone over seventy who had ever worn a uniform was dragged in front of the TV cameras or paraded before groups of schoolchildren.

In other cases, the celebrations became a moment for reflection or sparked off polemics. That is the case with the fiftieth anniversary of the destruction of Hiroshima (6 August 1945). The Smithsonian Institute in Washington is planning an exhibition with the title, "The Last Act—The Atom Bomb and the End of the Second World War." A number of veterans' associations have attacked the project, backed by the majority in Congress. The reason for the protest is that the exhibition is held to portray the Americans as aggressors and the Japanese as victims.

Such bickering apart, it is undeniable that the anniversary is a significant one. Commemorating Hiroshima is appropriate and instructional. But in most cases, anniversaries look as if they are just another trick dreamed up by copywriters and advertising agencies. It's not just an American phenomenon because Great Britain this year has celebrated the four-hundredth anniversary of Scotch whisky, the three-hundredth birthday of the Bank of England, one hundred years since the erection of the Blackpool tower, and the twenty-fifth anniversary of the TV debut of "Monty Python's Flying Circus." Nevertheless, the United States imbues its commemorations with an unmatched ardor and passion. You could say that America has been cruising along for some time now with its eyes fixed firmly on the rearview mirror. As any driver will tell you, this can be dangerous.

The most perverse manifestation of the trend is the upcoming tenth anniversary of the yuppy, the young urban professional, who was born at the age of thirty in 1984 (The Year of the Yuppy) and who passed peacefully away in the recession of 1990–91. Yuppies were officially christened by *Newsweek* magazine. On the cover of the December 31 issue, there was a cartoon by G. B. "Doonesbury" Trudeau of a young man in coat and tie on a racing bicycle and a woman in a suit with a briefcase and a personal stereo.

Those were the yuppies. Do you remember them? They were the spiritual children of Margaret Thatcher and Ronald Reagan, neither of whom is likely to have been aware of their existence. They were reputed to be sexually voracious, workaholic, ruthless careerists who were convinced that the Stock Exchange index would keep rising indefinitely and who spent their time in expensive restaurants, luxury automobiles, or exotic holiday destinations in a desperate attempt to squander an income that always proved equal to the challenge.

Today, yuppies are in vogue in Russia, Poland, and provincial towns in Italy. Here in the U.S.A., they are gathering dust on the shelves of fashion history, together with rockers, beats, hippies, and punks. Like those early computers, which are now sold at flea markets as collector's items, yuppies have stood aside to make way for this year's models. The buzzword now in Washington is *sappies*, or suburban aging professionals. They are quiet individuals who look after their gardens, cut the discount coupons out of the Sunday newspapers, and drink red wine or cappuccino. In 1999, they'll be celebrating their fifth anniversary. With a barbecue.

• • •

PERHAPS I SHOULD have realized at once that something significant was about to happen. Ninety-two-year-old senator Strom Thurmond confessed during an interview that he really only liked talking to good-looking young female journalists in short skirts. The woman who was interviewing him seemed amused. Two years ago, that would have been enough to start a protest campaign, or at least legal action. Certain things just weren't said in politically correct America (note the verb form—imperfect). The skirts of women journalists, until very recently, were no joking matter. And it didn't matter if you were ninety-two, fifty-two, or twelve years old.

Today, things aren't quite so cut and dried. The Republicans, after the mid-term elections, are back in power in Congress and political correctness is not the only victim in this summer of 1994. To understand the developments that could follow this changing of the political guard, it has to be remembered that Washington has been a Democratic town for forty years. The last Republican-majority Congress was in 1954, when *On the Waterfront* won the Oscar, someone called Hugh Hefner was launching a new magazine for men, Eisenhower was in the White House, and eight-year-old Bill Clinton had a crush on a girl in his class called Donna Wingfield. Since then, the Republicans have had their moments of glory. Ronald Reagan's 1980 victory was historic. But the House of Representatives, the true heart of the nation, remained impregnable. That is why the election result looked to many people like the end of an era, and not just a run-of-the-mill handover. "Mesopotamia. The Pharaohs' Egypt. Athenian Democracy. The Roman Empire. Byzantium. The Ming Dynasty. And now, Democratic Washington," wrote the *Washington Post*, (only half-)jokingly.

There's something else you need to bear in mind. Politics in the District of Columbia is an industry. The 535 congressmen (435 and 100) are surrounded by swarms of assistants, aides, researchers, secretaries, and lobbyists, all of whom spend money in the restaurants, laugh in the cinemas, chatter in the lifts, crowd the embassies, emerge from the taxis, and leave messages for each other on the telephone as they sow the only crop that will grow in the fields of Washington. Power.

While the Democratic party held the majority in Congress, most of these individuals were also Democrats. Not even a series of Republican presidents—Nixon, Ford, Reagan, and Bush—could alter this state of affairs. What in Italy is left to piracy and personal greed in America is strictly regulated. Patronage has been turned into the new frontier of science on this side of the Atlantic. There is a second rule in Congress by virtue of which the majority party, which appoints the chairs of congressional committees and sets the legislative agenda, has two thirds of the positions and the minority has the other third. "Positions" does not just mean jobs. It means physical locations, such as offices with a view (and a restroom), as well as bigger grants, more assistants, and, crucially, more places in the underground parking lots, over which epic battles have been fought.

For forty years, the Democrats had no objections to this practice. Now, the Republicans are enjoying their—exquisitely sweet—moment of revenge. And since we're in America, even this showdown has a festive side. It's a massacre under the glare of the spotlights that seems to inspire both victims and perpetrators ("I believe in getting my own back," said one habitué of the conservative Heritage Foundation). The last time the House changed hands, there were three thousand staffers. Today, there are twelve thousand working at the House and seven thousand at the Senate. And the Democrats can't even recycle themselves in the administration, which has cut back from one hundred and thirty thousand employees in Reagan's day to the present figure of fewer than forty thousand.

This earthquake on the Potomac—the Big One, if Clinton's expression is anything to go by—has done more than transform the staff on Capitol Hill, often known simply as the Hill. It is also revolutionizing hierarchies, habits, and personal tastes. For the winners are not the prep-school Republicans, George Bush–style GOPers from good families and even better schools. They belong to a new, vibrant race that flaunts red tartan ties and ruddy cheeks, and changes its automobile to come to Washington.

Lists of what is IN and OUT fill the newspapers. They shouldn't be taken too seriously because, after all, they are written by journalists in mourning (80 percent of Washington's press is of the Democratic persuasion) who are past masters at making inaccurate predictions.

One or two examples. Forrest Gump, the intellectually challenged patriot played by Tom Hanks, is IN but the ironically hyperviolent *Pulp Fiction* is OUT. Villas in Virginia are IN. Pretty little houses in Georgetown (like ours) are OUT. Prayers are IN at school while contraceptives are OUT. The singer Sonny Bono ("I

Got You Babe," 1965; former husband of Cher, elected with the Republicans) is IN whereas Fleetwood Mac and Barbra Streisand, who are too much at home in the White House, are OUT.

The conservative black judge, Clarence Thomas, and those who are defending him are very much IN while books supporting Anita Hill, who is still claiming she was sexually harassed, are on the way OUT. Chevrolet Suburban automobiles are IN and Volvo station wagons are OUT. Jogging is OUT, especially presidential jogging—even Clinton has been invited not to display his milk-white pedal appendages any more. The conservative *Washington Times* is IN while the venerable, politically correct, liberal *Washington Post* is OUT. The OUTest person of all at the moment is probably Hillary Clinton, whose ambitious program of health-care reform was, in many people's opinion, the real reason behind the Democrats' collapse. The First Lady's fans (she still has some) are worried. The way things are going, she might have to pull on a short skirt and interview a Republican senator.

• • •

WASHINGTON HAS MANY defects but it is a practical city, where conversation focuses on one simple, concrete question, "Who's in charge today?" So it's quite a shock to hear graying senators talking about the third wave, the psychosphere, and cy-berspace. Indeed, it is almost indecent how quickly the estab-lishment—urged on by the media, for whom decency is not a limiting factor—has jumped on the futuristic bandwagon. When Bill Clinton arrived and started jogging, the number of joggers multiplied. Now that the new star in the ascendant—Newt Ging-rich, the leader of the House and guru of the Bible-belt right—is talking like a new-age visionary, there has been an increase in visionaries. Washington is certainly a place that knows how to adapt.

Note that on the banks of the Potomac, "visionary" is not an insult but a sophisticated compliment. "Futurist conservative" is the current modish oxymoron. In other words, the Republicans have wrested the title of innovators from the Democrats, who only two years ago appeared to embody everything that was good and modern in American life. Newt Gingrich is spearheading the new movement. He lectures on subjects like "From Virtuality to Reality" and surrounds himself with futurologists, with whose assistance he is wont to prognosticate upon the nation's destiny.

The new high priests do not inspect the entrails of sacrificial animals to divine the future (that would be unhygienic, as well as politically incorrect). They merely propound bold theories (that are impossible to disprove, since they are about the future), such as the table that Michael Vlahos drew up to illustrate the new socioeconomic hierarchy of the twenty-first century. At the top of the heap, there are the Brain Lords (code for Bill Gates, the founder of Microsoft). Then come the Superior Services (today's professional classes) and after them the Industrialists, the Home Workers, and the Lost, or in other words, "the ones who can't make it."

Many of these modern-day mystics have written books that, at least according to the dust jackets, will open up new horizons for the human race. For example, Alvin Toffler has published *The Third Wave*, in which he explains how the world is passing from the industrial era into the age of information when a new T-Net (transnational network) will seek to find its Practopia (or practical utopia). The book—which your correspondent duly purchased for $6.99—is described by the publisher in the following terms, "The classic study of tomorrow. Sweeping across history and future, it reveals the hidden connections among today's changes—in business, family life, technology, markets, politics, and personal life. Identifying the directions of change, it has led American corporations to refocus their strategies, Japanese leaders to encourage their country's leap beyond industrialism, and Chinese intellectuals to press their campaign for democratic reform."

In this stimulating, albeit not particularly modest, environment, Newt Gingrich is completely at home. He has stated, among other things, that virtuality on the mental level is something that can be found in the leadership at various times in history, adding that, as in 1760, the English-speaking world is going through a transitional period with immense implications. In 1760, he explained, it was a passage from an agricultural society to an industrial one. Today, that industrial society is becoming information-based. These may not be the world's most original insights but they are almost orthodox in comparison with *The Third Wave*, which the leader of the House requires newly elected Republicans to read as part of their holiday assignments.

Some people think this craze for neologisms is a matter of language alone. The terms that fifteen years ago could only be found in video games or Talking Heads lyrics have made it into the vocabulary of the establishment, which is having fun trying them out. Yet, the new right is imbued with a slightly worrying messianic angst. Some of their initiatives are welcome and pleasantly ironic in tone, such as opening a website called Thomas (after Thomas Jefferson) so that people can follow what's going on in Congress. But their final aim would appear to be more radical. Newt Gingrich thinks of himself as a technological de Gaulle and intends to remake American civilization. Fine. Even if the civilization there already doesn't look too bad to this foreign visitor.

January

*W*hen you come back to Washington after a visit to Italy, it's nice to find America hasn't changed. The blue flowers are still flourishing defiantly in the front garden and the Stars and Stripes is still fluttering above the door of our student neighbors. Three rain-sodden copies of *The Economist* lie abandoned before our front door, and are transferred urgently to the radiator. The air smells of expensive logs burning in grates and the streets are littered with Christmas trees that have been mercilessly evicted after the festivities. I counted eighteen of them, in the block delimited by Thirty-fourth Street, P Street, Thirty-third Street and Volta Place, creating a bizarre horizontal forest that makes negotiating the sidewalk a challenging exercise.

In the package of post, which the local post office has held at my request, I find more proof of the holiday excess. My insurance broker sent me two birthday cards. The residents' association invited us to a holiday gathering at which festive dress was required (I would have liked to have gone, despite the dubious English). Du Bois Inc. of Georgetown had sent a holly-bedecked greeting card offering their preparations for winter, which range from cleaning gutters to the removal of birds' nests from domestic chimney pots. There was an interesting card from our neighbors at number 1526. They had invited us to a tea party, reminding us that it was their son's birthday, but also pointing out "that since it is not a birthday party (which will be held in June), guests are not expected to bring gifts." An invitation like that in London, I find myself musing, would put an end to most friendships.

Our Ford Taurus—the best-selling car in the United States, emblematic of America's middle classes and my own lack of imagination—is not where we left it. The towtruck has moved it to the other side of the road and decorated the windscreen with a (pink) twenty-dollar fine. A note pushed through our letterbox explains why. Residents were required to remove their cars from "the east side of Thirty-fourth Street between O Street and Volta Place, on the day of January 5, for the shooting of a major motion picture." In other words, they were making a film (adding that it was a major picture is one way of making up for the aggravation). The title was *An American President*, with Michael Douglas and Annette Benning. The only other film that ever hounded me like this was *Occhio alla perestroika*, with Ezio Greggio and Gerry Calà, which was shot in my hometown of Crema. It is, I suppose, progress.

The only really annoying thing about this new year is the weather, which is shamelessly warm. A few days ago, the thermometer registered seventy-two degrees Fahrenheit, or in other words twenty-two degrees Centigrade. The Americans, displaying a natural talent for striptease shared by all English-speaking communities, were going around half-dressed (it has to be said that their underwear, unlike that of their British cousins, was equal to the challenge). The women students in the house on the corner sit on the porch, drying their hair in the sun, and in the evening, they come out again for a smoke as if the porch were a seafront balcony.

You can spot the Europeans immediately for we are the only people wearing winter clothes. One or two of the braver ones go out without a scarf, so they tell me. Most of us, however, refuse to believe the thermometer and go by the calendar instead. We don't trust the weather. Washington's legendary winter is just around the corner and we are determined to be ready.

• • •

BRINGING A CHILD to America is a wonderful experience. It's not just that the whole country is designed for children—entertainment, services, food (ask your children which they prefer—a mushroom vol-au-vent or a hamburger and fries). The fun starts in Italy, as soon as you apply for a United States visa.

Much ink has been expended on the apparent lunacy of the questions applicants have to answer on the embassy form. No one, to the best of my knowledge, has ever considered the matter from the perspective of a two-year-old child. For according to the regulations, your baby has to make his or her application personally.

The questions regarding surnames or family names (1), first name and middle names (2), nationality (6), and other names (3) may present little difficulty but the subsequent inquiries begin to create the odd problem. It's fairly obvious that a two-year-old will not be married, widowed, separated, or divorced (question 13); will not be employed (17) or a student (18), unless that includes the first few days at nursery school. And since your baby hasn't learned to say anything yet, he or she will find it difficult to "indicate to a U.S. consular or immigration employee a desire to immigrate to the U.S. or purchase a U.S. visa lottery" (26).

But my particular favorite is question 29. Your child has to answer yes or no—perhaps by making a jammy thumbprint—to the following questions posed by the consular authority:

- Do you seek to enter the United States to engage in export violations, subversive or terrorist activities, or any other unlawful purpose?
- Have you ever unlawfully distributed or sold a controlled substance (drug), or been a prostitute or procurer for prostitutes?
- Have you ever participated in persecutions directed by the Nazi government of Germany; or have you ever participated in genocide?

There is one reassuring aspect. If the jammy thumbprint were to stray into the yes box, your child would have nothing to worry about. "A yes answer does not automatically signify ineligibility for a visa," the application form generously informs you.

• • •

ON THIS SIDE of the Atlantic, a child is an instrument of personal defense. In fact, I think children should be declared at customs as if they were weapons. When confronted with a toddler, cars screech to a halt, the most unattractive adolescents offer sweets, cooing shop assistants lean perilously across their cash registers, and passing acquaintances buy toys or rocking horses (we have an entire stable). Americans candidly admit that they "go gaga" over kiddies. My dictionary says this means they "become excessively enthusiastic."

Children—especially those between the ages of two and

four—enjoy absolute impunity in America. Let your small son loose in a university bookstore (I have actually done this) and everyone—students, faculty, and bookshop staff—will vie with each other to make him happy. Outrageous demands (a desire to embrace fifteen fluffy toy dogs at once) will be accepted as perfectly legitimate. Acts of underage violence (kicking the aforementioned toy dogs up and down the aisles) arc smiled upon. A neighbor called Karen who has just arrived from California—a formidable woman who jogs round the block sporting a cap with No Commitments written on the front—offers her three superb pedigree dogs in sacrifice every day. A child can stroke them, tease them, or chase them. Any grown-up that tried would be slapped unceremoniously across the face.

Public parks bring dogs and children—those two great American passions—together in harmony. At Montrose Park, which stretches from R Street to Rock Creek Park, dog-lovers and child-minders reign unchallenged. The adults present are slaves, there only to throw balls, push swings and lift toddlers (which means children who are too heavy to be called babies any longer) up to the top of the slide.

In the rare intervals when they are not on duty (their offspring may have found a puppy to play with), parents enjoy observing other people's children. This is not just further proof of the passion we have already mentioned. It is an opportunity for a comparative study. American parents, being American, are convinced that life is a race and the sooner you start running, the better. A playground is basically a place where you can keep tabs on the competition. British children tend to be thrown into the world like parachutists from an airplane—they're on their own—but their American equivalents are prepared with the care that professional mechanics lavish on racing cars. Every detail is crucial, and subjected to scrupulous attention, including sporting abilities, self-respect, dentition, and schooling. The message is that with sufficient planning and commitment, Nature can be improved upon. One way of achieving this result is to convince the child that he or she is absolutely unique and extraordinary. It is necessary to instill self-esteem, which means giving your offspring an inflated idea of his or her own importance as soon as possible. In Britain, one of the first words children are taught is "please." Across the Atlantic, they learn to say, "I'm great." An advertisement for a gymnasium I cut out of a newspaper carries a picture of an aggressive-looking infant and the slogan, "Give Your Child the 'Yes, I Can' Attitude.

This fanaticism blends in the parental psyche with the fear that one's child may not be up to it. In consequence, mothers and fathers obsessively monitor their children's growth and abilities. Here in Washington, there are exams for children as young as two and a half that are designed to establish a classification for entry to kindergarten. The youngsters are generally unperturbed but their parents are driven to the verge of a nervous breakdown. It is this combination of attitudes, mixing adoration, apprehension, and a total lack of discipline that ensures American youngsters will grow up as unruly despots with permanent smiles. The thought that sooner or later one of them will make it to the White House casts a cloud over my stroll home from the Montrose Park playground.

• • •

AMERICAN CIVILIZATION USED to have two great institutions. Your milk was delivered to your home and your newspapers were thrown vigorously at your front door. To find a milkman nowadays, you have to go through old magazine covers by Norman Rockwell but the tradition of the daily newspaper continues to flourish. The idea of starting the day without a paper is inconceivable to the universal middle class that peoples the United States. Dragging yourself out of the house half-asleep, and hoping you've got the right change, is not the way this great nation likes to begin its day.

Obviously, I adapted to the local custom. Every morning, I find lying outside my front door the *Washington Post* (in a transparent plastic envelope) and the *New York Times* (in a blue one). The service is reasonably priced and amazingly efficient. If you're going to be out of town for a few days, you just need to call a certain telephone number and deliveries are temporarily suspended. If your newspaper fails to arrive one day, call another number and a delivery car will bring you the missing issue in a couple of hours. In comparison with the Italian system of newspaper kiosks strategically located at road junctions where you can't possibly park, this is definitely progress.

But despite all this efficiency, many people in America are convinced that newspapers have entered an irreversible decline. Publishers are less worried by the fall in sales—down 20 percent on 1970 levels—than by the lack of new readers. Only half of today's twenty-year-olds read a daily newspaper, against two thirds in the sixties. The other half are glued to their TV screen or computer terminal.

Frankly, I wouldn't be so pessimistic. The smaller newspapers (85 percent of the total) are happy to write about a shooting, a bad storm, or a beauty contest but the big dailies continue to be excellent and, for the time being, essential reading. Younger Americans will discover this as they grow older.

We Italians, too, have several reasons to be grateful to them. To start with, they carry very little news from Italy, which enables us to digest our meals in comfort. Second, the major newspapers are "rooms with a view" on the United States. Take a look, and you will see the mind of America at work. The nation's conscientiousness, common sense, insights, enthusiasms, hang-ups, and obsession with being correct, which can lead to some extremely entertaining contortions, are all there in your daily papers.

Most of the Monday-to-Saturday daily newspapers are divided into sections, each with its own letter of the alphabet. The *Washington Post*, for example, has: A. News; B. Local news (Metro); C. Sport; D. Style; E. Business; and F. Home, food, and free time. Every paper has regular features, including columns by popular journalists, editorials, and detailed weather forecasts. There are features on all sorts of subjects from the media, gardening, and dealing with red tape to computers (there are two kinds of computer columns—those written by journalists who admit they don't know anything about computers and those by writers who appear to know everything).

For lazy readers, there are lots of tables, diagrams, and summaries. There are photographs for busy ones. And just in case there are any young readers—to show that printed media are not totally uncool—there are young people's sections, which usually annoy their target audience by treating them as if they were semiliterate or had recently arrived from outer space. Finally, in the belief that readers need cheering up, there are the cartoon strips. Some have been going on for years and on any given day the dialogue might go like this—Jack: "You shouldn't have done that, Donna." Donna: "Try to see it my way, Jack." (1249. To be continued.)

The adverts are really interesting. In Italy, advertisers tend to appeal to the buyer's vanity, trying to make him or her feel attractive, irresistible, and important (as if Italians had any need of such encouragement) but American ads all say the same thing. This product is great. Right now, it's a steal. So, buy it. To get the message across, advertisers fill all the available space with prices, discounts, addresses, and telephone numbers—in short, all the little details they can't put in a TV commercial. Many of the advertisements you see in Italian newspapers—for example, the half-naked hunk who appears to be making love to a can of spray-on deodorant—are quite inconceivable in the United States. They would be looked on as second-rate TV commercials and immediately forgotten.

One of my favorite corners in the *Washington Post* is the Weddings-Engagements-Announcements section that you get on a Wednesday in the Style supplement. It is a page in which all the formality of an apparently informal nation shines through. Every week, I am astonished at the photographs, in which the happy couple resembles a fifties' wedding portrait from provincial Italy. Why did Pamela let an unscrupulous lens merchant immortalize her with that pitilessly stark lighting? What is the reason behind Lieutenant McMahon's sinister smile? Who suggested that hairstyle to Tisha for her nuptials with Harry? But most of all, who wrote this account of the day's proceedings, "After the ceremony, a reception was held on the lawn looking onto the Ashokan Dam, where guests danced to the music of Betty MacDonald and admired the panorama."

Aficionados of these weditorials with literary pretensions will find further amusement in the confidential correspondence, where an anonymous agony aunt with a pen-name along the lines of Miss Good Manners answers readers' letters and solves their problems. This particular subspecies of journalism was imported into Italy many years ago, and has produced encouraging results. In their native land, however, such columns are vaguely pernicious. For while in Italy, a motherly Donna Letizia replies to queries that are basically reasonable (ranging from the importance of virginity to what cutlery to use for crème caramel), the American readers who sign themselves Desperate of Virginia or

Open Eyes from Missouri demand answers to questions that I can only call morbid.

After monitoring the *Washington Post* for a week (January is best month for such research), I ascertained that readers were worried, among other things, about: 1) what to do if your gun falls onto the floor while you are talking to someone in the living room (answer—pick it up); 2) how to react when your partner whispers something in your ear (answer—listen); 3) how effective molten wax is for mosquito bites (in January?); and 4) what to say when a houseguest arrives with three cats in tow. But the Query of the Week was, "How can you avoid complete strangers who want to tell you about their private lives in intimate detail?" Well, I'm afraid the only way is to leave the country.

• • •

BEFORE I CAME here, I had read hundreds of articles on American television as well as listened to thousands of comments (mainly from Italians who have never watched TV in the United States and even if they had, wouldn't have understood very much).

Nobody, however, had suggested a solution to this question, "Why is channel 20 on number 12 while channel 26 is on 6?" And why, in addition to being where they shouldn't be, do these channels have names like WRC-NBC, WJLA-ABC, WUSA-CBS, WTMW-HSN, WHMM-PBS, WETA, WFTY, C-SPAN, and ESPN? You even begin to miss Italy's mind-numbing Rete 4. It's that confusing.

The overcrowding problem is no laughing matter. In cities like Washington, the number of stations can only be compared to that in certain areas of Lombardy. The ancient Italian art of zapping, which is called channel surfing here, will make you dizzy but at least it convinces you that you really can find everything on cable U.S.A. There are channels like C-SPAN, which broadcasts what's going on in Congress so that the electorate can see the mess their chosen representatives are making of things. There are ultra-local stations that think a robbery at the Burger King has more news value than an earthquake in Japan. And there are the appalling shopping channels, peopled by vendors of suspect jewelry and ridiculous gadgets. (Who on earth is going to buy an umbrella with the Sistine chapel frescoes on the inside?)

The three major networks, which you can pick up with an ordinary antenna, are NBC (channel 4), ABC (channel 7), and CBS (channel 9). These have been joined by Fox (channel 5), which has exclusive coverage of American football. Public television (PBS), is on channel 6, even though this is numbered 26, and has no commercials (there are obsessive appeals for money instead), old British TV shows (costume dramas, documentaries, and so on), thoughtful political analysis, and popular children's programs like "Barney" and "Sesame Street." PBS is the only U.S. channel that could be mistaken for a European station. And so, when the kids have gone to bed, Americans watch something else.

It is no easy matter, I freely admit, getting used to American television. The enormous supply on offer induces a televisual version of the Buridan's donkey complex. Like the animal that starved to death when it had two equally desirable sources of food, you can't make a decision and so you end up watching nothing. It's therefore a good idea to find out how a typical TV day progresses on one of the major networks. You won't find out what to watch but you will learn what to avoid.

The day begins with morning programs (news, then junk). Then comes the afternoon schedule (just junk). At six o'clock, there's the early evening news (first local news, then national) and at seven there are the programs that will be copied in Italy ("Wheel of Fortune" and so on). Then from eight o'clock until ten, each network broadcasts four episodes of different serials, set in surroundings where the seriously overexcited are in the majority (newspapers, bars, universities, hospitals, or large families). The evening continues with a magazine program at ten and the late-night news at eleven, to close with the late shows, on which a celebrity anchorman (David Letterman or Jay Leno) interviews a fellow celeb and the audience enjoys finding out what great friends they are.

The most irritating thing about American TV is that it exists in a state of permanent agitation. The increasingly brutal ratings war and the shrinking attention span of the average viewer mean that every single program, from news bulletins to comedy shows, is a barrage of one-liners, sound-bites, and instant images. Talk-show hosts, actors, and reporters—with one or two exceptions—communicate weapons-grade anxiety as they fix the camera with a glassy stare and paper-thin smile, rattling off bursts of short, declarative sentences. Giuseppe Prezzolini, in his 1950 book *America in pantofole* (*America in Carpet Slippers*), noted the same phenomenon in the popular press of the day, "The superlative is the tuning fork that sets the pitch for newspaper prose and the incident, enhanced with picturesque detail, is inevitably transformed into the essence." Forty-five years later, little has changed. The difference is that today these crimes are committed in full color, and we can watch the culprit's mouth move.

It is not long, however, before newly arrived Italians find a few channels they actually like, and concentrate on those. Some go for sport (ESPN), others prefer news (CNN), or trials (Court TV), old films (Bravo, USA), documentaries (Discovery Channel), or weather forecasts (Weather Channel). A few refuse to relinquish the major networks and become regular viewers of investigative programs like "60 Minutes" and "48 Hours." Personally, I love the commercials. A few days ago during the Super Bowl, I saw one (an Italian would call it a *spot*) for Pepsi-Cola in which a boy ended up being trapped inside a bottle. A nation that slakes its thirst by drinking children—I don't know if you agree with me on this—is well worth studying.

An émigré's first impression is that American products will stop at nothing to show that they work. Scalpicin shampoo is not satisfied with a name that hints at summary torture and shows some poor individual in an office, his head white with dandruff, suffering devastating attacks of cranial pruritus. Indeed, to prove how effective their products are, manufacturers often resort to comparative advertising, something that Europeans find shocking. One automobile maker shows a rival car falling to bits. Another commercial has a fight between one trucker who is carrying Pepsi and another with a load of Coke. In the epic clashes of pills for headaches, constipation, indigestion, and flatulence (which to judge by the advertising has reached epidemic proportions in the United States), the sequence nearly always begins with some tormented soul refusing the proffered remedy and saying, "X isn't strong enough. Give me Y."

Another trick the commercials have is to promise viewers peace of mind. In the twenties, American adverts used to play on anxiety (Noxzema shaving foam is so named because it "knocks eczema"). In the thirties and forties, they moved over to power and technology (product names ended in -*master* or -*matic*). Today, there are hordes of deliriously happy families, friends sitting around drinking the same lite beer, automobiles with gently curving lines, and politicians who have suffered electoral setbacks (Mario Cuomo and Ann Richards) consoling themselves with potato chips.

Italian viewers are overcome by a sensation of drowning in

treacly emotion. It is as if the Italian Amaro Montenegro liqueur commercial had joined forces with Barilla spaghetti and Mulino Bianco cookies in a nauseating overdose of synthetic sentiment. But Americans appear to be immune to such reactions. Three hundred and fifty thousand commercials in the first eighteen years of your life, and seven hours a day per family in front of the tube, provide you with all the vaccination you need against the advertisers' excesses.

• • •

ONE OF THE habits I have kept up since coming to the States is listening to the radio. I have several strategically placed around the house, all tuned to different stations. Easy listening in the basement, to keep my spirits up. Classical music on the ground floor (which Americans, just to be difficult, call the first floor). And news programs in the study, the bathroom, and the bedroom.

This is not particularly original of me. Eight Americans out of ten do exactly the same thing every day. The average family has six radios, not counting the ones in their cars (that's why nobody steals them—there's no one left to sell them to) and the range of programs on offer—just like the variety of TV channels, breakfast cereals, and running shoes—is awesome. There are about 5,500 FM stations and 5,000 on the medium wave. In theory, I could change station every day for twenty-nine years. Assuming I survived the first month, that is.

The good old-fashioned radio is popular with Americans in these days of cutting-edge technology because it lets you participate. Foreign residents like it because it lets them listen to Americans participating. That's not true of other media. Letters to newspapers don't always get published. Not a lot of people make it onto television (even though there still seem to be too many of them). But the radio is open to everyone, and there are no filters. After the magic phrase—"You're on the air"—anyone can say what they want to. In provincial towns, call-in shows have turned into electronic city halls. Local affairs, from a polluted river to a proposed pedestrian crossing, are debated live, and no local administrator can afford to ignore the discussion. On other occasions, the target is Washington. When Congress voted itself a pay rise, many radio stations broadcast the direct telephone numbers of the offices on Capitol Hill, and the switchboard was jammed for days.

More than just forty years have passed since the days of Wolfman Jack in the film *American Graffiti*. A new age has arrived. The America that used to dream once needed disc jockeys. The America that protests today wants talk-show hosts. Some of them are famous, others less well known. Some are marvelous, others are dreadful. There are honest hosts who know how to listen and unscrupulous ones who use the so-called guillotine—when they get fed up with a listener, they put the phone down on them. Generally speaking, the dishonest ones are better paid and more famous than the honest hosts.

Not many talk-show hosts have made a name for themselves thanks to the even-handedness with which they conduct their programs. One who has, however, is Larry King (also helped, it has to be said, by wearing braces, or suspenders, when he appears on TV) and so have two young African American hosts, Derek McGinty, who works in Washington on National Public Radio, and Tavia Smiley from KMPC in Los Angeles, who has been included by *Time* in its list of Fifty American Leaders of the Future. Nevertheless, the talk-show stars are almost without exception angry, white rabble-rousers. Often their programs are networked across the nation.

The ruler of this particular kingdom is incontestably Rush Limbaugh (pronounced Lim-bawh), whose fame goes far beyond the confines of the radio. Ronald Reagan called him the number-one voice of American conservatism. Ruddy-faced and sarcastic, Limbaugh is a bullhorn bellowing out the frustrations of Middle America, who loves himself almost as much as he hates the Clintons. For Limbaugh, Hillary is a femi-Nazi and he long ago ran out of insults for her husband.

The explosive rise of AM/FM Democracy—with AM, or medium wave, on the political right and FM, or frequency modulation, to the left—has posed a number of problems. Unlike newspapers and television, radio is impossible to control. Protected by anonymity, callers sometimes spread false stories and make extremely serious accusations (that are never proved), which listeners will remember, just as they will forget the host's timid denials. Question: can the First Amendment, the one that guarantees freedom of speech, be stretched to include this Wild West of the air? The newly arrived foreign resident might be tempted to answer no, but sometimes it's better for such people to keep their mouths shut.

Second problem: do those who phone in, and manage in one way or the other to influence the national debate, form a representative sample of the population? Obviously not. Only one listener in a hundred actually telephones a radio station. But the ones who do call tend to phone in continually. They're known as the chronic cases, and after a time it's easy to spot them. Whatever the topic (from the Russian economy to skin diseases), they've simply got to express an opinion. And many radio stations ration the number of calls any one individual can make—one a month or one a week—to keep them under control. But the real hard cases won't give up. They camouflage themselves behind false names, accents, and identities. One local station, for example, is being persecuted by a listener who claims to be a well-spoken Mexican called Eduardo, or Elvis's gardener, or Hassid, an Iraqi-born taxi driver who is calling in to sing "My Way" because it's Saddam Hussein's birthday.

February

*S*now, at last. Eight inches of it, which is more than enough to make the TV announcers speak in contentedly alarmist tones and ordinary folk rush out to buy milk, bread, and toilet paper (they call it the nesting instinct, apparently). The newspapers carry articles that appear to have been written by elementary schoolchildren. Under headlines that say "It's snowed," women journalists with names like Terry or Marcia interview kids with sleds (carefully noting name, surname, and age), parents who are keeping an eye on them ("The kids are having a wonderful time"), snowperson artists who have been promoted to sculptors, and the inevitable fifty-year-old immigrant from Central America who has never seen snow before. I'm convinced it's always the same man from El Salvador who keeps moving round the United States, following the weather forecasts.

But being here when it snows is fun for another reason, apart from the fact that no one switches the air-conditioning on. The white stuff brings with it silent parks, adorning the cupid in our garden with an elf's hat of snow and uncovering a few interesting aspects of the American character. In London, snow is greeted enthusiastically because it constitutes a minor emergency (the British are specialists in emergencies). In Washington, it brings out the local passion for statistics ("It hasn't snowed like this for 1,410 days"), the love of forecasts ("From midnight to five A.M. four and a half inches of snow will fall"), the spirit of initiative (seven offers to shovel the snow from my drive in one morning) as well as an attractively childish side to ordinary people's personalities. Despite all the statistics and the forecasts, people are out to have themselves a good time.

And to have a good time, they don't need the designer spacesuits and state-of-the-art equipment that Italians can't wait to clamber into. A stout pair of shoes, a hat and a thick sweater is all that's necessary. It was in this spirit that we made a pair of blue plastic overshoes out of the envelopes the newspapers come in for our little boy, who didn't have any proper winter footwear. When we went out for a walk, the people we met congratulated us profusely. It seems the American winter just wouldn't be complete without an Italian toddler wandering the streets with the *New York Times* wrapped around his feet.

• • •

IF THERE IS one aspect of American life that has been put under the microscope and studied to death, it is the workplace. Think for a minute. Half the films you've seen in the past two years have been set in offices. The U.S. film industry makes a living out of career women and sensitive, caring men. Or sensitive, caring women and career-hungry men. Or sensitive women and caring men, neither of whom generally get anywhere in their careers.

But after ten months, I believe I can say without fear of contradiction that the films are little use as a guide. The few things I have come to learn about the world of work, I have understood thanks to good old-fashioned trial and error—which means learning from your own blunders.

• • •

IT IS NOW obvious to me that America sets great store by the title you have or the job you do. In Washington, the tendency is taken to obsessional extremes. When you're introduced to someone, they don't give you an innocuous, "How do you do?" They confront you with an aggressive, "What do you do?" to find out whether you're worth wasting any time on. Secretaries in the nation's capital have developed highly sophisticated ways of humiliating their fellow human beings, even though that old classic, "Please hold," is still their main standby. Two syllables that consign the caller to a telephonic limbo.

A flourishing industry has grown up around the passion for titles—inventing important-sounding names for very ordinary jobs. As I write, I have in front of me a collection of business cards that display an astonishing ability to bend the truth without actually lying. There is an impressive selection of vice-presidents who, to the best of my knowledge, have nothing to do all day, except perhaps exchange business cards with other VPs. My personal favorite in this category is the Philippine travel agent at the end of the street, who has appointed herself executive vice-president of Astral Travel. The woman in question works in a one-room "suite" with a poster of Bermuda on the wall. She was unable to tell me the time of the train to New York.

These self-styled tycoons have much in common with the bogus aristocrats who used to populate Italy. I have the cards of a couple of wives who have been promoted to bureau managers. Two hairstylists, who are merely ennobled barbers, four unspecified directors, several coordinators and advisors, hordes of sales associates (i.e., shop assistants), two used-vehicles representatives (which you and I know are really secondhand car dealers), and a semiretired senior editor I could hug.

The love of titles reaches its most exalted heights in the world of journalism. In comparison, we're amateurs in Italy. I know one or two people who work at the Washington weekly *The New Republic*, and I've counted on their management staff a total of thirty-three editors (including executive editors, senior editors, literary editors, managing editors, contributing editors, associate editors, assistant editors, assistant literary editors, and copy editors). I've only been able to find three journalists. If they're the ones who do all the writing while the editors sit around and edit, they must be slaving round the clock.

• • •

WHEN I'D WORKED out the rule about job titles—exaggerate, it won't cost you anything—I then realized that the love of appearances went beyond the words on a business card to embrace a whole series of social rituals. Working breakfasts and lunches in particular caused me one or two problems.

The easiest ones to deal with are often the most formal. This is because they have European models. One such is the Cosmos Club on Massachusetts Avenue, which can boast among its members several Nobel laureates. Essentially, however, it is a London gentlemen's club that has been uprooted and transported to Washington. The only difference is that the American club looks more genuine than the real thing. Perfection is of course the proof that the product is not original. The English, like the true artists they are, allow a little untidiness to creep in and blur the edges of the picture, as it were, thus rendering it impossible to reproduce.

It's just as easy to get by in the Italian restaurants. All you've got to do is say something in a strong Italian accent and make up one or two rules of table etiquette that no one will dare to challenge. As with the clubs, Americans are not content with copying. They want to copy well, and often manage to do so. Washington, so I am assured, has made stunning progress in matters Italo-gastronomic over the last few years. Some of the restaurants, such as Galileo, Café Milano, Filomena, Bice, I Matti, and I Ricchi (which is pronounced here as if it were *ricci*, Italian for sea-urchins), appear to have understood that non-Italians don't deserve the old caricatures of Italian cuisine, with their palate-scarring hot sauces and meat drowning in thick gravy. The original product from Italy is quite good enough. Other, less expensive and less well-known locales are equally praiseworthy, so don't let names like Thai Roma or Mex-Italia Rose put you off. The only real threat to your health is the waiter patroling the tables with a pepper mill the size of a bazooka. But he's like the rain or flu in winter. There's nothing you can do about it.

For Europeans, the difficulties start with the classic rituals of American life. For example, is it impolite, during a working breakfast, to stare at the sleep-starved eyes of the person sitting next to you and inquire what on earth made them get out of bed for this? At lunch, is it courteous to ask your American host not to keep passing her fork from one hand to the other like a juggler? The official explanation for this performance—that once Americans ate with just a knife in their right hands, which was used to insert food into the mouth—is one I find unconvincing. One hundred and fifty years ago, the residents of the United States had many other bizarre habits, like warring with the aboriginal peoples or shoot-outs in saloons, but they now manage to get along without them.

• • •

BUSINESS LUNCHES, I read in the introduction to a Washington restaurant guide, divide the city's population into four categories: power lunchers, hour lunchers, flower lunchers, and shower lunchers. The first group comprises influential people who discuss important business. Those in the second group are less powerful and only have sixty minutes to eat. The third are the seriously rich, who have plenty of time and flowers on the table. And the shower lunchers (from shower party, a gathering at which gifts are given to a woman who is getting married or having a baby) come in groups of ten, there is always one in the party who has something to celebrate, and they all ask for separate checks.

If we exclude the last category of fellow diners, who should in any case be avoided at all costs, one question will inevitably crop up on other occasions. Is it possible to order a beer or a glass of wine without looking like an unreformed alcoholic? The answer, I have come to realize, is not simple. Alcohol, once the fuel that drove public life in America and the lubricant that smoothed over the difficulties in any social relationship, is very much out in the nineties, at least in the presence of witnesses. In Washington, drinking beer at midday betokens a lack of seriousness. Allowing yourself a half bottle of wine is an admission of latent alcoholism. It's called "having a drinking problem" or just "problem." When it comes to covering up weaknesses, the British aren't the only ones who know how to juggle with the euphemisms.

One of the most attractive aspects of the Italian way of life—

the habit of consuming moderate quantities of alcohol with meals—is looked upon with suspicion in the United States. The youngsters who used to get so drunk at college that they couldn't tell a desk from a bed are now somewhat hypocritical adults. At working lunches, they shun the wine list as if it were radioactive. In the evening, they go back to their hotel rooms and ransack the minibar. At first, I used to get annoyed at this but now I will put up with horrors like hamburger and orange juice. Someone once wrote that "America turns any drug, from Martinis to art, into a question of public health and social morality." That's nothing. The problem is that we've now got to live with the consequences.

. . .

THERE EXIST IN America certain communications problems that have nothing whatever to do with language. One fairly banal example is physical distance. Two people talking in Italy will stand about half a meter (eighteen inches) apart. In Germany, they will be standing one meter away from each other, and in Great Britain as far apart as they reasonably can. In the United States, they will almost be making lip contact. When I first arrived, I merely put up with it but then I began to take countermeasures. Today, my conversations have become a sort of tango. My interlocutor advances. I back away, fearing halitosis and an unwanted opportunity to inspect the individual's most recent fillings.

Convincing one's acquaintances to maintain a safety distance is only one of the problems posed by communication and it is far from being the most serious. There is worse. After ten months, I have been forced to come to the following, disturbing, conclusion: When Americans ask you a question, they expect an answer.

Used as I am to the British, who make do with a snappy one-liner instead of a proper reply, and the Italians, who will tend to make a definite statement, I have often been at a loss for words.

Americans, I have decided, are ignorant of the art of conversation. The harmless social conventions of the Old World bewilder them. Here people simply don't realize that at a party nobody really wants to listen to what someone else is howling into their ear. In such cases, talking is only a way of keeping your mouth occupied and not eating too many olives.

Frequently, I have witnessed scenes like the following. Before dinner, a European is introduced to an American and asks a nice, general question, such as, "Have you been in Europe recently?" The American, who could be a professional, an academic, or a business executive, then begins to answer, explaining when he or she was in Europe. Where they went. What there was to see, and whether or not the experience was an enjoyable one. After a few minutes, the eyes of the European begin to wander round the room. (The French are best at this. No one lets their eyes wander the way the French do.) As a result, the American will interrupt the story but the wounded pride will be obvious.

It was with pleasure, then, that I read that certain communications experts have decided that such behavior is no longer acceptable. Because of differences in race, income, and age, American public discourse, according to these studies, is becoming verbose, emotional psychobabble and is headed down the road that leads to incommunicability. In short, Americans are moving round to the European way of conversation. Everyone talks. Almost no one listens.

Although this may look like a positive development—it would mean, for example, no more third degrees at cocktail parties—I must confess to having some doubts. It is hard to imagine such a practical, optimistic nation giving up discussing how to solve problems. This is the homeland of "Let's talk about it," the magical recipe of a country young enough still to believe in the miracle-working powers of the spoken word. The intricacies of Baroque rhetoric are unsuited to Americans. Woody Allen, anywhere in the United States outside Manhattan, might just as well be a Martian. He even looks a bit like one.

• • •

AMERICAN TELEPHONES AND European ones look, on the face of it, the same. This is partly because they are both often made in Japan. But the way the telephone is used in the two continents is very different. Not just because American phones work better and cost less. It's because in the States, the telephone is a means, that is, it is used to say something. Often in Europe the phone becomes the end. The aim is not to say anything but simply to be talking.

Staying too long on the phone is regarded as a sign of immaturity in America. A teenager can get away with it but not the teenager's mother. For Americans, the phone is basically a machine. It has not been invested with the moral and social connotations it has acquired in Europe. On this side of the Atlantic, everything has to be able to be done over the telephone. "Working the phone" is an expression that is almost impossible to translate into Italian (*lavorare il telefono* is unconvincing). It means having an objective and phoning around right, left, and center until you achieve it.

It is perfectly normal for an American to telephone ten stores to find out if they have a certain item before leaving the house. This behavior can be explained by reference to some of the characteristics of the country. Shopkeepers actually answer the phone. Local calls are paid for with a flat monthly charge. And the distances are enormous. Moving from one mall to another can be a major journey and it just wouldn't be worth it for the sake of a new shirt.

Nevertheless, Europeans won't accept this. They won't believe that the store has precisely the shirt they want. They won't buy things they haven't seen. An insurance policy taken out over the phone leaves you wondering whether you spoke to a ghost. A bureaucratic snarl-up solved over the phone might not have been solved at all. A French anthropologist has written that her fellow citizens are deeply convinced that to obtain anything at all you need to go in person. The same thing could be said of the Italians, some of whom are also quite likely to slip the clerk a sweetener.

Americans find this distrust baffling. On occasion, when I have phoned back for confirmation, and been recognized, the person on the other end of the line has been genuinely surprised. ("What's that? Didn't I tell you yesterday?") The life of the entire nation hinges on the phone, which has been simplified as far as is humanly possible. Every number has seven figures. Every area code has three. Americans can't understand why Rome has a two-digit code, Sassari's has three, and Vicenza's four. Nor do they see why there should be short (four-digit) and long (eight-digit) numbers in Milan. When I call my paper in Italy—area code and number, seven digits—the American operator always thinks I've forgotten some of the numbers. The only difficulty in America is making a long-distance call from a public phone. You need to have exactly the right change and get involved in detailed negotiations with the operator. But this is only a problem for tourists. Americans will either have a calling card, a telephone credit card, or make a collect call at the expense of the party they are ringing.

In my early days here, two phone-related phenomena left me

vaguely perturbed. One was the readiness with which acquaintances would say, "I can't talk now. I'll call you back." The other was the habit of phoning people at home (for work reasons, even people you don't know, and even at eight o'clock in the morning). The only thing that continues to irritate me is the eight o'clock caller, an individual beyond the pale of civilization. Calling people at home, whether they are distinguished academics, public officials, or my insurance agent, is something I've got quite used to doing.

A word of warning. This willingness to answer the phone does not show that America is a relaxed, informal community. It proves instead that protracted phone conversations are unusual. You don't mind answering the phone at home because you are unlikely to be kept on the line for half an hour. In the States, no one over the age of four plays silly games like, "Guess who-o?" Here, people don't use the telephone to engage in an emotional workout, or take a windcheck on the state of a friendship, or see how quickly you react. A brief exchange of pleasantries and then it's down to business.

To return to the world of work, family and health matters are not avoided in initial greetings, as they are in Great Britain. I have in the past had occasion to call an official at the State Department who justified his lengthy absence by describing in detail his own particular case of arthritis. This apparent friendliness sometimes tempts us Italians to go too far. When we do, we are punished, for as we are embarking on our own enthusiastic tale, another phone call will usually arrive and we will be on hold for the next five minutes. The vital thing is to realize what is happening in time, otherwise you may have to go through the entire routine again.

A final note. While Italian telephone manners have barely emerged from the Stone Age (represented by those who ring up

and ask, *Pronto, chi parla?*—"Hello, who's that speaking?"),
America is racing ahead with new technology. At the cost of drop-
ping some horrendous clangers, I have learned that:

- When you hear the signal for an incoming call, it is
acceptable to put your current interlocutor on hold for a
short time (unless it happens to be the president of the
United States).
- Lying about where you are calling from is not only
rude. It can be dangerous. The Caller ID service lets you
read the number of the person calling you. Another service,
activated by the sequence *69, lets you call back automatically the person you have just been speaking to. Unless, of
course, they tapped in *67 before your number when they
called you to disable the service.
- It is not impolite to use your answering machine to
check incoming calls. It's annoying when other people do it
to you, though.
- It is advisable not to leave on other people's answering machines (or in your own recorded message) funny
quips, squeals, riddles, or weird music. As we have said,
the telephone is a tool to be used for work and everyday life.
In any case, Americans haven't got a great sense of humor.

• • •

I ARRIVED IN this country convinced that political correctness—all the precautions one has to adopt so as not to offend
women, ethnic minorities, and everybody else who feels like taking offense—was a joke. After ten months, I have discovered that
it is actually a joke, but there's more to the story.

The phrase *politically correct*, which has been fashionable for a number of years now, means two different things. The first interpretation is "avoid all implicit discrimination in the language you use." The second definition is much simpler and less controversial: "be polite to others."

The former kind of political correctness has led to excesses, and media-fueled reactions, that prove that America may well be a fascinating country but it is full of people who love telling their fellow human beings how they should behave.

This neoconformism deserves all the ridicule it has attracted and I am certainly not going to defend it. Only a fanatic would use *womyn* instead of *women* to avoid the male chauvinist sound of the syllable *men*, prefer *Superperson* to *Superman*, or opt for *waitron* to eliminate the distinction between *waiter* and *waitress*. Equally, I have difficulty in believing that anyone wanting to avoid the adjective *black* would talk about the African American leader, Nelson Mandela, who is, in any case, South African. Or that there are people so irresolute as to want to eliminate references to Indians and the like from the names of basketball or football teams. The Washington Redskins are safe, for the moment.

I take a firm stand against such extreme views. They'll have to torture me before I call an elderly person "chronologically advantaged," a bald person "differently hirsute," or a homeless individual "involuntarily domiciled." Those who hope to impose such expressions are not just fanatics. They are deluding themselves. Neologisms like these will never catch on because they fly in the face of what we have seen is the first commandment of the American language: Shorten and simplify. In America, polysyllables are about as popular as nettle rash.

There is, however, a more reasonable side. Since it is less desirable, it tends to get less attention but for the majority of Americans, a minimum of political correctness is merely being polite. To put it another way, avoiding the words *short* or *fat*, especially in front of individuals afflicted by the conditions, is a question of good manners. The British have a similar way with words. All the short people in the British Isles are automatically promoted into the category of not very tall. The unpleasant are merely not very nice and the fat are frequently referred to as "robustly built" or "generously proportioned."

On other occasions, things aren't quite so straightforward. The subject of ethnic origin, for example, always has me in difficulty. I have no objections to calling blacks African Americans, or Indians Native Americans. Other words have come and gone in English and Italian before *black* and *Indian*. In 1953, for example, Guido Piovene wrote about his contacts with the *negri* of Washington. He would select another word today. But I do refuse to give up the adjective *white* in favor of Caucasian. I have never believed that we whites have any reason to think ourselves superior but I don't see why we should get the most embarrassing name of the lot.

These American obsessions (the late flowerings of Puritanism, perhaps?) are not in any way scandalous. Sometimes, however, they verge on the grotesque. Asking whether a necklace you fancy is a product of Native American craftsmanship makes the desire to acquire it evaporate. The same thing goes for the syntactical contortions that are necessary to avoid making the subject of the sentence—thankfully, in Italian you can often simply leave the subject out—only masculine. Here's an example from a newspaper article: "Who is the ideal candidate? He (or she) should be experienced. His (or her) reputation, untainted. And he (or she) should be bold." This has to be done even if there are no women candidates. You never know.

It is an arduous and—let's face it—depressing task to have to do without so many comebacks and snide remarks. In America, as I have come to see, you are well advised not to joke about the following subjects: sex, race, and death. Once you have forsworn these topics—the juiciest sources of humor—you can try to smile about anything else you like.

The British simply don't understand this determination to go without so many of life's little pleasures. A funny funeral joke is still one way to make a good impression in polite London society. But Americans will have none of it. Political correctness, as we have noted, inhibits them on the subjects of race and sex. And when it comes to the Grim Reaper, there is an unspoken but widely held belief that death is optional. If only the subject were studied in sufficient depth—and not joked about—then it might not ever be necessary to shake off this mortal coil. And here practically minded U.S. publishers have found a gold mine.

That leaves the mentally ill. But here, too, the hunting season is over. American humor on the subject of mental illness—where it exists—is entirely involuntary. According to *The Diagnostic and Statistical Manual of Mental Disorders* (a million copies sold of each edition), the number of such maladies has increased in only fifteen years from 106 to 333. The list appears to include every human activity that is not positively health-enhancing. And so we find nicotine abuse and caffeine intoxication, defined as the "recent consumption of caffeine usually in excess of 250 mg (more than 2–3 cups of brewed coffee) followed by restlessness, nervousness, excitement, insomnia and flushed face." There's the disorder of written expression, whose symptoms are "grammatical or punctuation errors within sentences, poor paragraph organization, multiple spelling errors and excessively poor handwriting." As things stand, I won't ever be able to say to my fellow journalists that they drink far too much coffee, smoke like a chimney, and write abysmally. Since they'll be suffering from three distinct mental disorders, I'll have to treat them with kid gloves.

To sum up, foreigners should avoid going to extremes and looking ridiculous. But it's wise to get to know the ground rules so as not to embarrass anyone. Remember that American embarrassment isn't a fleeting shadow that, British-style, barely darkens the brow. It is highly visible and very audible. In fact, it always has been.

A nineteenth-century English traveler, Charles Janson, addressed a maid during his stay in America using the appellative "servant." The young woman was not impressed. She replied, "I'd have you to know, man, that I am no sarvant. None but negers are sarvants." She went on to inform the stranger that she was the landlord's help. The story is an example of proto—political correctness. It shows that the (white) servant's hour had come. African Americans would have to wait. Janson, the inconsiderate traveler, is the archetype of contemporary visitors from Europe, who risk saying something untoward every time they open their mouths. A robust Italian accent, in some circumstances, means forgiveness in advance.

March

*O*ne American critic maintains that books on Italy by foreigners fall into one of the following two categories—the chronicle of an infatuation or the diary of a disappointment. Description of America by Italians, I am firmly convinced, run the same risk.

Over the course of his or her own highly personal investigations, every visitor develops a certain number of fixed ideas with which to badger family, friends, and acquaintances. The founder of this idiosyncratic school was an Englishwoman, Frances Trollope, who penned her wickedly barbed *Domestic Manners of the Americans* in 1832. On the eve of my departure, here are my own American obsessions—in addition, of course, to the earlier generalizations. They can be conveniently, and alliteratively, collected under the letter C:

Control, Comfort, Competition, Community, and Choreography

CONTROL

One of the basic phrases of American English is *to be in control*. The Italian equivalent is not *controllare*, a transitive verb that leaves the listener expecting an object. (Keep what under control? A car? An erring partner?) The phrase implies to have the situation under control. Any situation. From your health to the weather, your bank account or phone bill. An itemized phone bill, which in France is considered a scandalous invasion of privacy, is the norm in the United States. Americans need to know that when they called their friend Al in La Jolla, California, at 8.23 P.M. on 2 July, they spent $2.26 for a sixteen-minute conversation. Italian phone bills—at best, an act of faith on the part of the consumer—would start a second Revolution.

This passion for control has been interpreted in a number of ways. It has been said that this is proof of America's Teutonic roots, tempered by Anglo-Saxon common sense (58 million Americans claim German ancestry, 39 million Irish, 33 million say they are British, and 15 million Italian). And there is some truth in this. Northern European practicality is evident in all American behavior. It is the spirit of criticism, which many Southern Europeans think (wrongly) is the only form of intelligence, that leaves a little to be desired.

You don't have to be an anthropologist to notice a passion for order and predictability. You only have to look around. Preachers and dieticians offer salvation in five easy lessons. The party that cut its manifesto down to a shopping list and inserted it into the TV guide won the elections. The author who published *The Seven Habits of Highly Effective People* is now a millionaire.

A British journalist has written that manuals of this kind—and two thousand new how-to books roll off the presses every year— are one of America's most original contributions to the nonfiction shelves of the world's bookshops. So what? How-to books date back to Benjamin Franklin, who was always quick to spot a market niche. They prove that this is a nation of optimistic self-improvers, convinced that happiness is above all a question of mind over matter. And they also demonstrate that Americans reject the idea that success comes all at once, without effort, or luck, or a guardian angel, or an influential relative.

Often, Italians mistake this attitude for naïveté, or superficiality. But what it reveals is a love of precision and a desire to stay in charge of one's own life. One American woman I know has programed everything, month by month, for the next three years. Moving house, pregnancies, births, and holidays. She's an intelligent person and is perfectly well aware that you have to factor in the unexpected. But she's tidied all that away into a little pile, like the Community Chest cards in a game of Monopoly, and contentedly carries on planning. That's why the letters that friends and relatives exchange over the year, which are often printed and oozing with good news and success stories, are not written with the addressees in mind. They couldn't care less about Cindy's promotion, Chuck's haul of athletics medals, that great vacation in California, and the dog's continuing rude health. The letters are really intended for the people who wrote them, who are thus able to look back on their recent lives, and pretend they were in control.

COMFORT

America's second lesson can also be boiled down to a single word—*comfort*. To Italian ears, the word suggests old-fashioned tour brochures and package holidays (*L'albergo dispone di tutti i comfort*, "the hotel has all mod cons"). But in American English, comfort just means being comfortable. It's one of those paths to be trod in the pursuit for happiness, a right enshrined in the Declaration of Independence (the right to pursue, that is, not the right to happiness itself).

Take clothes. When Italians get off the plane, they have to deal with a whole series of incomprehensible rules. *Casual* in the United States has nothing to do with the sophisticated coordinates that go under this name in Italy. American casual is much closer to the word's etymological roots—garments picked at random and worn without reference to any guiding principle, except the utter, unimpeachable, overriding contentment of the wearer. It's no surprise that the cotton industry is enjoying its biggest boom since the war.

An attractive aesthetic effect is, at this point, irrelevant. Even unpleasant body odors, which terrorize most Americans, become a matter of opinion. Clothes sizes acquire a philosophical dimension. At the National Press Club a few days ago, someone told me that sweaters were only available in L and XL sizes. "But what about people who aren't large or extra large?" I inquired. The sales assistant, who was firmly in the latter category, looked at me as if I were a bondage freak who enjoys squeezing into a straitjacket.

Pernicious casual-mindedness has imbued with new relevance Clemenceau's celebrated one-liner that America is the only nation in history that has passed directly from barbarism to decadence, without the usual interval of civilization.

The president of the United States jogs through the city in shorts that display to the world his milk-white thighs, and T-shirts that announce the imminent arrival of his fiftieth birthday. The CEOs of major corporations present themselves in public in shirts that suggest a particularly laid-back lumberjack. Employees, taking advantage of a new fad for dress-down day, turn up in clothes and shoes that are open to a certain amount of criticism. On airplanes, the striptease performed by America's fliers before takeoff, justified by the need to get comfortable, has become an intriguing source of entertainment. Not even gangsters, *Newsweek* noted recently, wear a jacket to work any more.

In general, the media seem to be as relaxed about these new habits and clothes as the wearers. They find excuses on moral grounds (America hates deceit), cite historical precedents (Woodstock, hot pants, Madonna), and point to irreversible trends (only 13 million men's business suits sold each year). Grunge, born in Seattle and inspired by adolescent anti-fashion, has contributed to the self-absolution, lending the phenomenon a patina of intellectual respectability. Five years ago in America, it was possible to be shabbily dressed but nowadays you're grunge.

Some people have been digging into sociometric statistics to justify this trend. Working women with children (19 percent of the total in 1960 and 60 percent today) have neither the time nor the inclination to worry about the way they look. They go from their two-piece suit and off-white tights (code name, power suit) straight into their husbands' sweatshirts. It has to be said in passing that this habit makes the Eastern United States a strangely sexless land. Physical perfection is tolerated but feminine fascination is a no-no. Or rather, it is restricted to Hollywood films, where excess of any kind—even an elegant woman—is held admissible. In a book called *Sex and Suits*, the fashion historian Anne Hollander puts forward a disturbing theory—the decline of formal wear in America may be irreversible. Once, butlers wore wigs and the master dined in tails. The tails were then handed down to the butler and the master donned a dinner jacket. In restaurants today, it's the maître d' who wears the dinner jacket while the patron turns up in a jacket and tie. When the head waiter starts turning up in jacket and tie, diners will be munching away in T-shirts, before they discard even those.

So, it's that easy? No way. Just when you think you've understood the rules (number one: everyone can do their own thing; number two: kids are born in sneakers and never take them off), perfidious America raps your knuckles. The government and civil service opt for white shirts, starched as stiff as an ironing board. The pale blue preferred by Italians is considered daring in Washington and the striped shirts worn in London are viewed as decidedly eccentric. There are white bow ties galore at gala dinners and first nights. And that is the punishment meted out to Italians in the United States. We are either overdressed or underdressed. Never are we dressed appropriately.

COMPETITION

One evening, the computer I am writing this on decided to pack up. The image on the monitor froze, failing to respond to any command key. Since it's an Apple, I phoned 1-800-SOS-APPL (1-800-767-2775). I was greeted by airport-style Muzak and then a voice cut in. Its owner could not have been more than sixteen but there was nothing about my computer he did not know. He guided me step by step (switch off, reboot, press this, click that), occasionally scolding me and asking me questions I couldn't answer. But ten minutes later, my computer was purring back to life. Oh, and since it was a 1-800 number, the call was free.

My experience with Apple was far from unique. Over eleven months, my cris de coeur went out to a wide range of companies, including Panasonic, Ford, Bell Atlantic, American Express, and

Mattel. All we foreigners do it. Customer service is our lifeline in the stormy ocean that is America and everyone has fond memories. We all love telling our minor success stories. One Italian diplomat told me of his nocturnal encounter with General Electric, whom he called when his refrigerator began to make suspicious noises. The technician on duty gave him the third degree, obliging him—among other things—to stick his head inside the errant domestic appliance and report back on what he could hear. In the end, it turned out that the distinguished diplomat's fears were exaggerated. The fridge was merely defrosting itself.

Why do these services work in America? Because if they didn't, the public would simply look for others that do work. Competition is more than a healthy economic precept, it is a moral imperative (in the American anatomy, the heart is never far from the wallet, and vice versa). Actually, competition goes a long way to explaining the excellence and excesses of the country, including the efficiency and Byzantine complication of the phone system, the abundance of television channels and the number and financial instability of the airlines. For consumers, competition brings (almost) only benefits. There are a few exceptions, such as lawyers, universities, and hospitals, which are outstanding, numerous, and breathtakingly expensive.

Back in Italy, we often have no, or a very limited, choice. There's one airline for Milan-Rome flights while for Milan-London, where there are two, both charge exactly the same prices. If you want to phone Rome, London, or anywhere else in the world, you have a choice of just one phone company, which does exactly what it likes with you. When we come to the United States, we can actually decide. An Italian in America is like a child let loose in a toy shop. I know of one who spent days conducting a personal auction with AT&T and MCI, the phone giants, negotiating terms. Obviously, he knew he was only one among tens of millions of customers. But he felt important. His buck was going to the best offer, but it would have to be earned.

COMMUNITY

Robert Putnam, a prominent Harvard scholar and occasional advisor to Bill Clinton, has revealed that the president regards Italy as an example of a civil community that the United States should imitate. Please resist the temptation to say, "I see why Clinton is in trouble now." Let's try instead to ask ourselves, "Is it true?"

Before we attempt to reply, we shall explain Putnam's—and apparently, Clinton's—point of view. His argument is that the United States has ceased to be the land of associations that fascinated Alexis De Tocqueville a century and a half ago. People today have forsaken civic engagement and social activities to shut themselves up in their shells. The hedge, not the open prairie, is the emblem of the new American dream.

In recent years, membership has been shrinking at the Lions, the Red Cross, and the Scouts. Ordinary people continue not to vote or join trade unions. Even the recreational social activity par excellence, ten-pin bowling, has been affected. While the total number of bowlers has risen by 10 percent over the last four years, the country's bowling leagues, the groups where bowlers play, chat, eat, and drink together, have suffered a 40 percent decline. The inevitable conclusion is that Americans continue to go bowling, but in pairs or on their own (Putnam's article was in fact called, "Bowling Alone").

It has to be said that this scholarly thesis, while undeniably intriguing, is less than convincing. This is a country that was founded by refugees who would not tolerate restrictions. When they landed in the New World and ministers of religion began to tell them how to behave, the new arrivals scattered across the entire continent. Great Britain, not the United States, is the home of the team spirit. When Margaret Thatcher tried to change this facet of the British national character and ordered her fellow citizens to behave like Americans, telling them to get rich and beggar their neighbors, she might as well have started counting the pigs flying over number 10 Downing Street. She'd probably have had more luck.

But going back to America. This nation of individualists is not above uniting its forces from time to time. In 1993, 89 million Americans—half the adult population—were involved in some form of voluntary activity. This means that while some associations are in decline, others are coming into being to meet new needs. Religious groups and PTAs are on the increase. And what are gangs if not new examples of coordinated, albeit criminal, activity? As indeed are the neighborhood watch groups that have sprung up in response. If Tocqueville were ever to pay another visit, he'd be impressed.

And Italy? To point to us as examples of civil engagement is extremely flattering, but a little out of place. I don't have up-to-date details of Italy's neighborhood committees and parish social centers but I get the impression that they're not exactly in the best of health. The associations that work in Italy are based on individual interest (co-owned apartment buildings, bridge clubs, and sports supporters' bars) or are driven by fashion (the recent boom in political groups, for example). In Italy, the ideal association has a president, a vice-president, and two directors general. Mum, Dad, and the two kids. Such associations—and I'm sorry for Bill, here—cannot be considered examples of civil engagement. But in Italy the family is still central and, at least in comparison with America, still works fairly well.

CHOREOGRAPHY

I'm so glad I'm livin' in the USA!
(Uh-huh! Oh, yeah!)

CHUCK BERRY

Just try that with France, Switzerland, or Germany instead of the USA. No one is going to start singing *Ich bin so froh, in der Bundesrepublik Deutschland zu leben!* to show how great it is to live in Stuttgart. And above all, no one is going to chip in with a chorus of *Uh-huh! Oh, yeah!*

There are many reasons for this passion for America, most of them perfectly justified. There is, after all, no accounting for taste and if some people love the USA on account of peanut butter, that's their problem. Defining the attraction of America has long been a hobby with Europe's intellectuals (you'll find a couple on every package holiday, sitting in the front seats of the tour bus). Their verdicts include: People like America because of its size (the roads, the deserts), or its modernity (Manhattan, Los Angeles), its efficiency (transport, telecommunications), or the many images of America we carry around in our heads (Coca-Cola, Mickey Mouse, McDonald's).

But one aspect of America is difficult for Europeans to stomach. I've been trying for the past year but still without complete success. That aspect is America's choreography. The residents of this country are convinced that anything good has also got to be over-the-top, in-your-face, and ear-splittingly loud. We might call it large-scale wanton tackiness. As it is voluntary, there is no judging the phenomenon. And since it is universal, there is no escape.

The hero figures of this America are Mae West, Liberace,

Muhammad Ali, Joan Collins, and Ivana Trump. Larger than life personalities who at first sight, and often at second or third, are beyond comprehension. How can they like that stuff? The sacred places of this America are Las Vegas, Atlantic City, every bar in the state of Texas, and every swimming pool in California, as well as 90 percent of official ceremonies and any sports event you care to mention.

Not long ago, I watched Americans getting excited about the show they put on for the football Super Bowl in Florida. It was a gigantic reconstruction of Indiana Jones fighting with Ancient Egyptians. What has Indiana Jones got to do with football? What has football got to do with the Ancient Egyptians? What have the Ancient Egyptians got to do with Florida? Absolutely nothing at all. But together they made quite a show, and that was justification enough.

A few days ago, I was watching a basketball game with a friend. I asked him how the ultra–politically correct United States could embrace, as it were, both feminism and cheerleaders at the same time. The answer was, "Feminism is right. Cheerleaders are good-looking." Then he borrowed my binoculars. I'm pretty sure he wasn't checking out the progress of feminism.

• • •

THIS SMALL AD appeared on March 19 in the Unfurnished Homes column of the *Washington Post*, more or less in the same spot where we had found our home a year earlier.

GEORGETOWN—Charming, bright house.
3br, 3 ba, study, lg garden. Mrs Webb.

We noted that in the course of the year, our house had acquired a luminous personality (it was now bright) and a study while losing a little grace and half a bathroom. It was still charming, though. We braced ourselves for the rush of prospective tenants, which failed to materialize. After a few days, a metal notice was set up in the garden, as agreed in the contract, announcing that the property was FOR LEASE. The notice, and the introduction of our home's details into a databank, had some effect. Curious individuals began to turn up at the door. Not aspiring tenants, who generally look normal enough, but Realtors, Washington's real-estate agents, many of whom, we decided, needed an eye kept on them, particularly if they were anywhere near the silverware.

Some unctuously proffered business cards that claimed they had once been lawyers, in some former incarnation. Others presented themselves without an appointment, trailing lost-looking Mexican clients in their wake. One was called Chip. In contrast, prospective tenants were vaguely embarrassed because, in a certain sense, their poking about in our bathroom and opening our walk-in closets was an intrusion into our lives. They had no idea that we were intruding into theirs.

Over three weeks, we witnessed an intriguing parade of North American fauna. We met seriously large students who had difficulty in squeezing through the doors. Lovers who rushed straight indoors to check out the size of the bedroom. A New York academic who wandered around for half an hour without taking his mackintosh off, like Peter Falk in "Columbo." There was a Democratic congressman from Florida who told us he loved the house. His wife, unfortunately, said she didn't feel comfortable. Where she came from, she said, every room was as big as our entire house and residents had a square kilometer each to park in. Georgetown, she implied, was not for her.

We began to break camp, the prelude to moving house proper,

as the first flowers bloomed and the first breaths of spring air-conditioning began to blow. These operations posed no real difficulties, although obviously service companies prefer to gain a customer rather than lose one. Unhurriedly, in only a few days, we closed our bank accounts, handed in our credit cards, and canceled the cable TV subscription. An ethereal voice trilled that Bell Atlantic would disconnect our telephone number one hour after we had left and the final bill would be forwarded to Italy. The car insurance, the *New York Times*, and the electricity company promised to send me (dollar) checks with refunds. I look forward with anticipation to cashing them at my bank, and spending one hundred thousand lire in commission for two hundred thousand lire's worth of American currency.

We sold the car with its imitation leather interior. We handed the furniture back to its legitimate owner (we had repaired one drawer and reupholstered one of the armchairs). We invited Dave, Greg, and the other students from New England for dinner, to thank them for humbling us with their wisdom for the past year. We gave away a box of toys to a girl called Lora. It was only when we announced our intention of holding a yard sale, the American way of getting rid of excess baggage before moving house, that Patty Webb, the agent-cum-mother who stayed with us to the end, shouted, "Oh my God! I've got to buy a camcorder!"

• • •

THE PROBLEMS POSED by yard sales are the ones humanity has to face every weekend—money, rain, and unwanted guests.

The initial expense is the cost of publishing a five-line announcement in the local paper for three days, Friday to Sunday. Thirty-seven dollars. In other words, if the takings amount to less than thirty-seven dollars, we might as well not have bothered. The weather is another imponderable. In springtime, Washington can discover an unsuspected desire to be in the tropics and drown your merchandise in a torrential downpour. But the real problem is the clientele. A yard sale, by definition, is open to the public and in America, the public includes some truly remarkable specimens.

Our yard sale should have started at ten o'clock on Saturday morning. The first customers rang the bell at eight, pretending to have misunderstood the announcement. Of course, they had read it extremely carefully for these were the legendary early birds, intent on reviewing everything on offer in case there was anything of value. Our ultra-naïve advertisement for a Back-to-Europe sale was for them an irresistible siren-song. Hungry-eyed couples. Silent traders. Breathless joggers, pretending they were trying out the armchairs. A colossal African American with two gold bracelets insisted on buying my phone for twenty dollars. Help arrived just before I gave it to him for nothing.

We had made careful preparations for our yard sale, which for Europeans in America is rather what a ride in a horse and carriage is to Americans in Europe. Slightly silly, but unavoidable. As well as making the newspaper announcement, we had hung notices on the trees on Thirty-fourth Street. This amused our neighbors hugely, who arrived en masse and bought nothing. The women undergraduates of Georgetown proved more interesting, both from the aesthetic and the commercial points of view. Miniskirted and determined, they carried off all our lamps and kitchenware. The beds were acquired by an officer of the U.S. Marines, a student about to emigrate to Israel, and a family of immigrants from Indonesia, who blocked the traffic for half an hour trying to lash their purchases to the roof of their car.

Over the course of the day, we had about one hundred visitors.

Roughly thirty made purchases, spending $325. Many behaved oddly. Two came down the stairs on bicycles. One descended kicking a soccer ball. One well-dressed lady arrived with her maid, ordering her, "Choose." A couple of young women bought a side table and then demanded I take it apart and fit it into their subcompact automobile. At least ten people wanted to buy bits of the garden, including the sundial, one of the plants, and the little cupid. In the afternoon, a perfect stranger arrived with a schnauzer on a leash and told us he hadn't been able to come earlier because he was in the stable with his horse.

But the people I found most intriguing, and my wife most disquieting, belonged to two distinct categories, the ones who talked too much and the ones who said nothing at all. The former bargained furiously, prompting me to rediscover the childish delights of standing behind a shop counter with a brass-neck lamp and a notebook for jotting down receipts. The others—the mutes— came, looked, ignored my greetings, and trawled through the carpets, phones, and writing desks with a reproachful mien. Some wore earrings (in their ears or in their noses) while others were leather-clad titans, with dark glasses and ponytails. Hollywood has taught us that people who dress like that are unpredictable. They might hand over a million dollars, turn into werewolves, or pull a gun on you. With the latter two possibilities prominent in our minds, at dusk we counted our takings, padlocked the gate, and declared our yard sale officially closed.

• • •

I REMEMBER WHEN I arrived in Washington a year ago we had admired the cherry blossom and watched the Japanese tourists photographing each other furiously under the trees. We went back to see them again. This year, there were dozens of street vendors mingling with the Japanese tourists and the cherry trees. Overhead, kites flew.

After queuing up with the Russian and Ukrainian visitors, we finally visited the White House. We saw the Rose Garden, that famous fireplace, and the Oval Office (through the window), all places I had never been able to penetrate as a journalist. Secret Service agents patted down our toddler's stroller, affixing a stylish badge with the legend THE WHITE HOUSE—STROLLER NUMBER 347. It's no coincidence that tourists from Odessa find it easier to get into the White House than do journalists. It's all part of the great show that is the US of A, and I rather like it.

Even in these—our last—days in America, we have found out new things. We've learned that the best pizza is from Domino's, the deep dish one with extra cheese and fresh tomatoes. We have realized that this country of so many watery beers does produce one exquisite brew (Samuel Adams) and an excellent ice cream served with a biscuit (the legendary Klondike, whose symbol is a polar bear). We've even found out where the brightness and color contrast buttons are on our old wood-effect TV. So, Americans aren't flustered and red in the face when they appear on the box after all.

It's not unpleasant to be closing the cycle of the seasons. The senator's wife is venturing out into the open again, and took the opportunity to yell at our removal van ("Get away from there right now! I'm a senator's wife!"). A blood-red flyer invites us to take part in the Volta Park Spring Cleanup. I glance at the date and note with satisfaction that I will be eight thousand kilometers away. Eggs and bunnies are taking over the shop windows, although no one knows why rabbits should be a symbol of Easter. The pansies on the front lawn have resumed their struggle with the Atlantic winds and Washington's dogs. The birds under the gutters, blissfully ignorant of summertime, are once again in full voice at six in the morning.

We take advantage of a sunny day to picnic in the garden again. My geraniums have succumbed to the cold but the white-blossomed dogwood tree is budding vigorously and the magnolia looks ready to dump its tons of leaves in the neighbor's swimming pool again. The mild winter has left the ivy green and healthy. Only the concrete cupid still looks like a concrete cupid. It continues to pour imaginary water from its concrete jug and waits, like America, to become old.

Postscript

Five Years Later

*T*hey've moved the cupid. It now stands on a pedestal in the midst of four rose bushes that keep a respectful distance. Actually, the cupid now has a rather mischievous air. Perhaps he saw the thieves who removed the fountain from the garden. He may have been watching the presidential elections. Or it could just be the same expression the cupid had before, and I'm imagining the rest. When you've turned forty, revisiting the past is a dangerous game.

This house in Georgetown, number 1513 on Thirty-fourth Street, is where I lived in 1994 and 1995. It was here that I constructed my very own, personal, America, starting at the bottom. In my case, this meant a basement with a "Happy Days"–style kitchen and a dining room straight out of a John Grisham novel. The kind they lock the hero up in, and no one is able to find him again. The first floor was more welcoming, with wood floors, two fireplaces, and windows looking into the garden. The concrete cupid stood in the garden. When I left, he was waiting to grow old, like America. He's done his best, I'm sure. But like America, he's still going to have to work on it.

The house has been sold to an American couple, Patrick and Adam, who own a store on Wisconsin Avenue that sells objets d'art. I got the news from Patty Webb, the real estate agent and substitute mother who took us under her wing when we arrived, our two suitcases full of useless paraphernalia and our heads full of confusion. Ms. Webb is one of those steel-hard women that America once manufactured in huge numbers. She buys, sells, administers, and rents homes in Washington. Her Achilles' heel is that she becomes genuinely fond of her clients, especially when they pay the rent punctually and refrain from shooting out of the windows. Patty is very proud of the success of *Un italiano in America* (the original title of this book). She's been told that a number of readers have turned up on the doorstep of number 1513. Several have taken photographs. One or two have even rung the doorbell. Ms. Webb is enormously entertained by all this. Perhaps the new owners are less delighted but I'll find that out very soon.

The house we are staying in today is about four hundred meters from 1513. It has been lent to us by two friends, Kerry and John, who are holidaying in Europe. To get to it, all you need to do is go down Thirty-fourth Street, skirt Volta Park, and turn right into Reservoir Road. The building, in red brick, is at number 3337 and enjoys a commanding view of the street. Leading up to the front door is a small, ivy-smothered flight of steps, attractively framed by flowers. Every morning, the newspaper carrier, with impressive precision, slings a copy of the *Washington Post* at them. And every morning, the flowers, bruised but unbowed, determinedly haul themselves erect again. On Sundays, the papers weigh as much as a small car, and the flowers take a little longer to recover.

At the back is a handkerchief-sized garden boasting a remarkable concentration of convalescent vegetation that Kerry has entrusted to our ministrations. A note on the door of the refrigerator—all communication in the United States takes place on fridge doors; the Internet is merely an extension of the basic principle—announces a visit from the minions of the Merrified Garden Center (motto, "Twenty-nine years and still growing"). The gentlemen concerned turned up the day after our arrival. Three Salvadorans who asked us questions about plants we'd never heard of in a language we couldn't speak. They clearly would have preferred to be somewhere else. Comprehensively jet-lagged myself, I regarded them with affection. Some things in America never change.

• • •

OTHERS DO, HOWEVER. For example, Washington seems to have recovered its health. There's a new mayor, crime is down, drug use is down (or perhaps people are just using different drugs), and the middle classes are moving back into town. You can see that fresh money—from the 'Net economy—is circulating. The adolescents who in the mid-nineties were hunched over computers in the garages of Virginia and Maryland are now assessing investment opportunities and thinking seriously about buying a home. These young monied whites are slowing down a flight from the city that has been going on for twenty years. In what was once known unofficially as Chocolate City, African Americans are today a majority in decline. I read in the *Washington Post* that the District of Columbia has half a million inhabitants, classified as follows—318,657 blacks, 150,854 Anglo-whites, and 38,453 Hispanics. It is not clear into which group Italians fall. We're not blacks. Neither are we Anglos. Quasi-Hispanics, probably. In that case, we're going to have to work on our pronunciation of *nachos*.

At first glance, Georgetown has changed less. The neighborhood is still green, fragrant, and appealingly démodé. In the time it takes to demolish and reconstruct three buildings elsewhere in the city, here they might manage to change a door handle. Not the lock, though. When Americans colonize Mars, their door locks will still be cumbersome and difficult to open. Flowers, whose care is delegated to the residents' sense of civic responsibility, decoratively circle each tree. Yellow Ryder's vans shuttle student kitchenware into the houses around the university. The nearby staircase where *The Exorcist* was shot continues to attract frisson-seeking film buffs. The disused tram tracks, ever ready to slash a passing car tire, have a more lustrous sheen now that they are safeguarded from any modernizing impulse by a preservation order. The year's big news story is exploding manhole covers. What happens is that now and again a cast-iron manhole cover will leap into the air. It is not known why they do this but residents find it stressful.

As I walk along Thirty-fourth Street, I discover that Volta Park now lives up to its name. Railings have been put up and the sidewalk I weeded with such gusto looks as if it has been relaid. Sprightly dogs race across the grass, their owners panting after them. I recognize one of my former neighbors, Karen, with Potemkin, her pocket-sized canine companion. She tells me that a lot of people in Georgetown know about *Un italiano in America* and have been trying to locate me. I resist the temptation to ask her why and inquire instead about local news. Karen tells me she has moved, the summers are less torrid, and the senator from Montana has bought a Harley-Davidson. Nothing much has changed, she concludes.

I'm not so sure. Even in this fragrantly perfumed corner of the States, a new wind blows. The signs of dotcomization (from the dot.com website suffix) are unequivocal. The Internet has brought money to the area and changed people's routine. When we first arrived here in spring 1994, we would invite friends to dinner using the rudimentary CompuServe e-mail service. At the table, we would talk of little else. Today, the computers that glow through every window—which still have no curtains—are busy ordering pizzas on-line, even though it's much easier by phone. There is a web address on every advert. Even the plastic bag that enables the *Washington Post* to fly more aerodynamically toward our long-suffering flowers invites us to "pay all our bills with OnMoney.com."

At my feet, Mrs. Bettina Conner's three dogs lift their aristocratic muzzles. At any moment, I expect them to let out a heart-rending cry of "wu-wu-wu," but they don't. They look me over, and trot back to Volta Park.

• • •

I MAY HAVE the house keys in my pocket but this time I'm here as a tourist, so I can permit myself one or two little indulgences. I've rented a convertible that used to be white, and is now impregnated with the unmistakable odor of rented convertibles everywhere. The smell is a mixture of cigarette smoke and exhaustion, left behind by all the forty-year-olds who have rented it for the weekend to ride around in a baseball cap.

After amusing myself for a while with the foldaway roof, and nearly decapitating the other members of the family, I look for somewhere to park. Not an easy exercise, but an unavoidable one. The parking inspectors are as inflexible as they were five years ago, so if you don't have a parking permit from the police, you have to scurry outside every two hours and move your vehicle. The only parking spot that is always free is in Reservoir Road. It's under a tree that drips a sticky substance onto the windscreen, making it difficult to see out. A bee in a jar of jam would see the world much the way I do from inside my Chrysler convertible. But a bee doesn't have to drive to the police station and apply for a parking permit.

. . .

POLICE STATIONS IN America have one big advantage. They look like American police stations. Hanging around in them is fascinating for anyone who has ever watched an American TV serial. You see cops packing pistols as big as some Italian police officers. And you see mothers who don't know whether to be angrier at their children or the officers who have arrested them. But we only came here for the parking permit that residents can temporarily transfer to their houseguests, thus sparing them a succession of heavy fines. Nevertheless, there is no statutory entitlement. The police have a certain number available and when they run out, you have to join the queue. We Italians have, however, realized that a number of different police stations can issue permits for the same zone. If the first station has run out, you might be able to find one somewhere else. That was how we embarked on a big-game hunt that involved phone calls and car chases across the city. If ever you see a convertible screeching to a halt outside a police station in Washington, it will either be the FBI or an Italian houseguest checking out the parking permit situation.

After a number of false starts and red herrings (public services always give you an answer in the USA, even if it's complete non-sense), we finally obtained our Visitor Parking Permit for George-town, which we would have to display on the dashboard. Proud of our achievement, that is precisely what we did. We then proceeded to buy the groceries, forgetting that we had rented a convertible. When we returned to the car, the permit had disap-peared. After exchanging the usual recriminations, we went back to the police station, where a kind-hearted sergeant made a pre-tense of scolding us, issued another permit, and suggested that we shut the roof when we park. We smiled, promised, took our leave, and exited.

Back in the car, I ordered my son, Antonio, to say nothing. But he was trying to work out which Pokémon figure looked most like the sergeant, and didn't even hear me.

· · ·

MARX IS DEAD. Patty Webb, the mother hen of an agent who comes to see us from time to time to make sure we are in good psychological health, bearing eagerly accepted gifts for Antonio, has told us that the legendary plumber, cynosure of our first American sojourn with more than eighty years—and even more phone numbers—on the clock, has finally shuffled off this mortal coil. I am truly sorry, for it was he who five years ago accused me of illegal plumbing practices when I asked him for a stronger shower head. Not that you need one at number 3337 Reservoir Road. The shower there could pin Bruce Willis to the opposite wall and runs a serious risk of reducing to a soggy pulp the books that Americans like to keep in the bathroom. My personal favorite is *Political Insults Throughout History*. For every insult, I can think of an appropriate Italian politician.

• • •

IF WE NEED anything, says a Post-it from Kerry on the refrigerator door, we can ask Ching or Aida. For a week, no one made an appearance, which led me to conclude that the names were mere fabrications. Then on our last day, someone turned up brandishing the front door key. Since the woman concerned had no Italian, and very little knowledge of English, I deduced that this must be Ching. We duly solicited her approval with gestures. Ortensia, my wife, was worried that the cleaner might spot a microscopic scratch on the parquet floor. I hoped she wouldn't read the prices on the products in the refrigerator. They were all from the Fresh Fields supermarket, one of Georgetown's two exciting new retail adventures (the other is the Barnes & Noble bookshop on M Street). Yesterday, we managed to spend more on shopping for dinner than it would have cost us to eat out. And, as Antonio remarked when we got home, all the stuff was still raw.

Fresh Fields is a temple to the cult of American alimentary correctness. When I picked up a flat peach and asked if it was genetically modified, a solicitous assistant hurried to explain that it was only a "doughnut peach." At Fresh Fields, the produce is organic, biological, and telegenic. And they have prices to match. Safeway, which in 1995 was for me the last word in shopping chic, now looks like an unassuming Standa store back home. In contrast, Fresh Fields is for intellectuals. Young women with a studiedly disheveled air diffidently observe vegetables that could give them lessons in dress sense. Athletic advocates leap like mountain goats from a white Californian wine to a French red. Pubescent youngsters with earphones drift round the counters (which are brimming with free samples—we could have solved our dinner problem without going home), swaying to the rhythms of mysterious music. Their particular hobby is making salads, upon which all the associative fury of the U.S. consumer has recently focused. The combinations are profoundly disturbing. Asparagus and asphodel. Cashews, carrots, and coriander. Gruyère and gelatin. Shrimp and sprouts (of soya or, indeed, any other plant that dares to grow under American skies).

Other products enable me to understand the progress America has made in gadgetizing its home life. I came within an ace of purchasing a Charcoal Companion, a thermometer to introduce into your barbecuing steak to find out how well it is cooked. I let perfect forks and superbly designed knives nestle neatly in my palm. I had a go on the centrifuge for chilling wine and beer. There was even a little table with the precise times required to induce 1) moderate lip chapping (chilly); 2) frostbite of the palate (cold); and 3) necrosis of the oral cavity (iced). Annoyed, I took a quick look round for someone to try out a little thermal provocation on. I wanted to scream, "Why is your beer always too cold and your coffee too hot?" Then I realized that the sophisticated clientele at Fresh Fields might actually have agreed with me. And where's the fun in that?

• • •

THIS RETAILING REVOLUTION, I reasoned, is bound to have produced at least one casualty. The small store on the corner of Thirty-fourth and Dent, the one people in Georgetown call Old Grandfather because it's always been there. "Always," you might object, is not a very American adverb. And you'd be right. So let's say that this particular corner shop has been there as long as any of the residents can remember. That's a long time. Almost forever.

Five years ago, only one student was allowed to go in at a time as a space-saving and anti-shoplifting strategy. No dogs. And no exceptions. In a place like this, a Dalmatian puppy could nibble a hundred dollars' worth of merchandise without moving. The store was so narrow that customers often did their shopping in profile, as if in some surreal Egyptian mural. It was the antithesis of spacious suburban malls. A store like that couldn't have survived, I mused. It must be a boutique selling Italian pottery by now.

But I was wrong. Old Grandfather is still there. The door is still narrow and the neon signs still hang in the window. And at this moment, two workmen are hammering away at the door and window frames. Inside are the ranks of an orderly army whose soldiers are biscuits, lightbulbs, tubes of toothpaste, wine, beer, and lip salve, a sure indication of the nation's optimism (if chapped lips are a serious problem, everything else must be going reasonably well). I approach. Elbow resting on the newspaper stand, the owner looks me up and down. His name is Huday Yavalor, and he is Turkish. He introduces me to his assistant, an Iranian who can sing Peppino di Capri's popular hit, "Roberta." Huday explains that he has to change the windows, hence the enthusiastic hammering. I observe that it can't be easy selecting the range of products to sell in such a small space. You have to know precisely what your customers want. He looks at me and pronounces solemnly, "It's tequila season." The assistant nods his assent. We stand in silence on the corner of Dent and Thirty-fourth, an Italian, a Turk, and an Iranian reflecting on what all this might mean for the future of America.

• • •

BACK AT THE house, I came across a catalog called *Restoration Hardware*. Naturally, it has nothing whatsoever to do with restoring things, or with hardware. Instead, it is a collection of objects from the thirties through to the sixties, all sold at Y2K prices. A glance reveals that these are very special articles. They are what is known in the United States as icons, which is a sort of honorific. "Well done," the title says, "you have been useful and become part of our lives. We shall not forget you."

This is American classicism, and we should not scoff. Gertrude Stein wrote that Americans are the "materialists of the abstract" but, in my opinion, they are more like abstractionists of the material. Only in this way could one explain how the collective imagination has absorbed the Big Wing juice extractor ($55), or how the Silver Swan fan ($129), launched in 1934, still stirs something deep in the American soul. Perhaps a cocktail of Chandler and Hammet, with illustrations by Hopper and Rockwell, as they think of Marilyn Monroe and listen to Glen Miller.

I examine the Thermo King ($18), with its dull aluminium body and red-plastic-handled top. When the Cunningham family from "Happy Days" went for a picnic, they would certainly take one of those with them. I discover Resto Nos. 2, 4, and 6 flashlights by the Bright Star Company, a model that dates from the early sixties. Prices, from the smallest size to the largest, go from $10 to $14 to $19.50. The caption says, "The perfect flashlight for camping, repairs and walking the dog at night." I look at it more closely. It is the classic flashlight. The one that children all over the world draw. Every other flashlight is a deviation from this norm.

In the catalog, there are also photographs of pots for mustard (yellow) and ketchup (red), selling for $1.95 each. There are LP frames ($26), in which fifty-year-olds can display (and periodically substitute) their memories and their melancholy. The cover features the Road Trip Set ($10), a plastic model car with a canoe on the roof (the classic station wagon), and trailer (the detachable trailer). This object is a replica of a toy that was popular in the late forties when America, having won the war, joyously hit the road. It is still out there. The Road Trip Set is such an unsophisticated toy that even the most stimulus-deprived infant would toss it aside in disgust. But Americans have come the full circle. They are now back where they started. It's as if, having filled the bathtub of their lives to the brim, they were now pulling the plug. After constructing an endless succession of increasingly sophisticated household objects, they now seem to yearn for Edenic simplicity. It's a back to basics movement that savors not so much of surrender as of anesthesia.

. . .

AMERICAN COURTESY HAS always fascinated me. It's an automatic weapon that slips the safety off with an innocent-sounding, "How are you today?" before letting rip with a burst of, "Great to see you!" "Take care!" "Have a nice day!" "Have fun!" and "Missing you already!" Many visits to the United States, and a long stay, have convinced me that nothing and no one could resist firepower of this magnitude.

But I didn't think it would be the Americans who changed. The courtesy is still in place but they've lost their enthusiasm. Today, politeness is just social lubrication. I realize this when I use the phone for the twittering voices of the switchboard operators are now an octave lower. In gas stations, my hesitation at the pump (do you lift the handle or push it down?) produces more irritation than laughter these days. Practical America is now impatient and has told courteous America, "Let's get a move on."

To understand just how much the atmosphere has changed, you need only take a walk along M Street. The aggressively friendly waiter at Old Glory, the one who told you the history of his family as he served you a hamburger and stood watching you eat your fries, has been replaced by an efficient professional. "Why do I have to smile," his eyes say, "if you're going to leave me my 15 percent tip anyway?" At the Vietnam restaurant in Georgetown five years ago, they would answer your questions, albeit laconically. Now, they're down to monosyllables. At the new Barnes & Noble bookshop, they serve the most lip-searing coffee known to humankind. If you object, they look at you with barely veiled eyes and murmur, "Wait till it cools." Down at Banana Republic on the corner of Wisconsin Avenue, customers are abandoned to wander among the heaps of discounted T-shirts. The sales staff, perfectly camouflaged, are indifferent to their presence. Only the jingle of the cash register will arouse them from their apparent hibernation.

All this is even more obvious in the local shopping mall, that hell-like heaven on earth and magnet for Italian tourists. In the GAP store at Pentagon City, which is not the place where generals buy their stars but a shopping center on the other side of the river in Virginia, the adolescent assistants wear headsets with a fitted microphone. State of the art, no doubt, but the upshot is they only ever speak to each other. The overall impression they convey is of mild autism. You may be wandering around, waving a pair of underpants and wanting to know if they are the right size, but if the sales assistants are busy exchanging mysterious messages about the availability of some product or boyfriend, you will simply get ignored.

Out on the roads, you have the final proof. The facial muscles of America's car drivers have finally tired of smiling. It has to be said that it was never easy to travel by car in the United States. The generous proportions of the road surfaces and the sheer simplicity of the rules have dulled drivers' ability to react. No errors or exceptions are allowed. If you slow down, they attach themselves to your rear bumper. If you're too slow getting into the right lane, they don't let you through. The rugged pioneer sense of owning the land has been extended to modern highways. Our habit of driving in the middle of two lanes, on the very Italian principle that you never know which will turn out to be the right one, provokes insults and raised tempers on the roads of the United States.

As I cruise round the Beltway in the wrong direction and cross two states to go from Bethesda to Georgetown, I muse, we go too far, too often. But someone ought to remind these Americans that they're not driving on railroad tracks. However, I keep my musings to myself. If I repeated them at a dinner party, the reaction would be so frosty that the roast would have to go back into the microwave.

• • •

KERRY, OUR AMERICAN friend, left us a note. "If you need anything, ask the neighbors Anna and George Gordon, the ones who live in the house with the flowers." As indications go, this one is at best vague. It's rather like saying, "They're the ones who live in the sunny house." In Cairo. All the houses in Georgetown have got flowers that vie with each other in the brilliance of their color and the pervasiveness of their fragrance. Still, we manage to find out where the Gordons live after a few days and duly ring the bell. Anna is an American woman of the old school, friendly and exuberantly outgoing. I think she came from Trinidad originally. She raises funds for the Democratic party, is interested in art, and has married a lawyer with a beard but no mustache, who also bears a striking resemblance to the former presidents on the country's banknotes. You'd get the urge to spend him if he wasn't so exquisitely polite.

We don't actually need anything. We just popped round to say hello. But Anna Gordon is not the kind of woman who's going to let things go at a plain introduction. We are obliged to return for dinner before we go home and so, the following Sunday, we are back again. The house is full of paintings. Classical music plays softly. The hostess is a fund of anecdotes. And when we reach the sweet course, she casually informs us that she was once a famous Bunny for Playboy. As we smile uncertainly, an illustrated book materializes, *The Bunny Years: The Surprising Inside Story of the Playboy Clubs*. In it, the lady of the house is portrayed in all her leporine glory, with tights, bow tie, and long furry ears. Even Antonio looks up from his Pokémon cards at this point. It's not every day you meet a bunny granny.

Anna insists that we keep the book, which has been signed by Hugh Hefner and several of her former colleagues, including the model and actress Lauren Hutton, Gloria Hendry, one of the James Bond girls, and Deborah Harry, better known as the singer with the pop group Blondie. She then tells us about the time the Playboy Club hosted the novelist James Baldwin and Woody Allen, who was introduced to Anna as "a young comedian who's going to go a long way." Her lawyer husband listens and smiles. We thank them. As we take our leave, I give them an Italian-language copy of *An Italian in America*. I explain that it, too, is a personal story. It's just that I was wearing different clothes.

• • •

THIS IS THE story of an Italian who, with his family, was happy in a house in America. We may be leaving but the house is still there, only four hundred meters away.

I decide to ask the new owners if I can take a final look round.

I stroll down Thirty-fourth Street, find the familiar white façade and ring the bell on the black front door. Patrick (or Adam) comes to open it. I introduce myself. I ask if they would please let me take a quick look round the house, or at least say hello to the cupid in the garden. Adam (or Patrick) smiles weakly. He says, "I know who you are," and suggests that I call back in half an hour. He'll have to speak to Patrick (or Adam). After wandering round the block, checking the window of the dry cleaner's, and soaking up a little rain, I go back and ring again. Adam (or Patrick) is no longer smiling. "Sorry. We cannot readmit you."

I look at him, and turn to go. No problem, Patrick (or Adam). The house will still be ours. You have only bought it.

Acknowledgments

THANKS TO INDRO Montanelli for what he has taught me. Thanks to the pioneers I never met (Giuseppe Prezzolini, Mario Soldati, Guido Piovene, and Luigi Barzini) and to all those—Italians and non-Italians—who have written more significant books than this one on America. Thanks to Orfano Sannita for his good advice, and to David Cornwell for the gnomes.

Thank you to the entire cast of Thirty-fourth Street and those Americans who, for an hour or a year, allowed themselves to be spied on and pretended they didn't notice. Thanks to the following friends and acquaintances—Daniel and Gaby Franklin, Patty and Bob Webb, Christine and Jack Giraudo, Sylvie Kauffmann, Richard J. Higgings, and to Joe DiMeglio and John Marx, my improbable muses. Thanks to Pam for the furniture, to Karen for the update, and to everybody who gave us a rocking horse. Kerry and John Parker lent us their home for ten days in the year 2000. It is to them that I owe the final chapter.

Some of the Italians who have opened their homes and/or hearts to me prefer the comforting blanket of anonymity (I understand). However, I would like to thank Stefano Ronca, Magda and Enzo Miranda, Sabina Bertolotti, Massimo and Anna Crovetto (the heroes of the Fourth of July), and Silvio Marchetti, who, as usual, had it all worked out. And thanks once again to Ortensia, a splendid companion throughout these adventures. I have forced her to move house nine times in eight years, and she's still smiling.

Illustration: Chris Riddell

ABOUT THE AUTHOR

Beppe Severgnini is a columnist for *Corriere della Sera* and also writes for *The Economist*. His books, published by Rizzoli, have been bestsellers in Italy. *Inglesi*, a portrait of modern Britain, was first published in 1990 and was followed by *L'inglese. Lezioni semiserie*, an entertaining and unusual approach to the English language. He is also author of two travel books (*Italiani con valigia* and *Manuale dell'imperfetto viaggiatore*) that examine the Italian national character through the behavior of the country's tourists. His autobiography, *Italiani si diventa*, published in 1998, describes the coming of age of his generation during the sixties and seventies. He was born in Crema, northern Italy, and educated at Pavia University.